STEVE WINWOOD:
roll with it

*by chris welch
with steve winwood*

A PERIGEE BOOK

Perigee Books
are published by
The Putnam Publishing Group
200 Madison Avenue
New York, NY 10016

First Perigee Edition 1990

Library of Congress Cataloging-in-Publication Data

Welch, Chris, date.
Steve Winwood—roll with it / by Chris Welch with Steve Winwood.
p.   cm.
ISBN 0-399-51558-5
1. Winwood, Steve, 1948– .   2. Rock musicians—England—
Biography.   I. Winwood, Steve, date.   II. Title.
ML420.W58W4   1989   89-16383 CIP MN
782.42166′092—dc20   [B]

Printed in the United States of America
1   2   3   4   5   6   7   8   9   10

This book is printed on acid-free paper.

CONTENTS

Above: On tour, September 1986. *(LFI)*

foreword

"Another damned, thick, square book! Always scribble, scribble, scribble! Eh! Mr Gibbon?" This was the reaction of H.R.H. The Duke of Gloucester on receiving a copy of Volume II of Edward Gibbon's *Decline And Fall Of The Roman Empire* from the hand of the author.

Another Gloucestershire resident, Steve Winwood, was rather less disparaging when I presented him with the manuscript of this account of his life and times. Perhaps not as broad in scope as Mr Gibbon's tome, nevertheless it represents a wide ranging study of the work and achievements of one of contemporary music's most respected and well liked artists.

In compiling the story I received invaluable help. I would especially like to thank Steve for his patience and courtesy in answering my many questions and for supplying welcome pints of real ale! I'd also like to thank Eugenia for her hospitality and generous assistance, and John 'Nobby' Clarke for help, information and encouragement.

Special thanks are due to Spencer Davis, Muff Winwood, Peter York, John Glover and Jim Capaldi and to Sian at Virgin Records, and Rob Partridge at Island Records.

Thanks also to my wife Marilyne for coffee, proof reading and cries of "Get on with it" and to my editor, Chris Charlesworth at Omnibus Press, for rather more urgent entreaties to complete the task. Incidentally, although Gibbon may have written *Decline and Fall* with a quill pen, at least he didn't have computers to cope with. Just a few moments before putting the finishing touches to the book my editor announced he wished to close an office window. He rose from his seat, tripped over a lead, causing a bright blue flash and an explosion which blackened his hand. At the same instant the computer screen went blank. It seemed likely the entire book had been lost in a catastrophic accident and two years' work had come to nought. Silently we carried the machine to another room, plugged in, pressed keys and, lo – there was the story of Steve Winwood, glowing green. Scroll with it!

Chris Welch, June 1989.

STEVE WINWOOD

CHAPTER 1

roll with it

"This song is very dear to me . . . 'Back In The High Life'." A wave of emotion greets Steve Winwood as he introduces this most crucial song at The Royal Albert Hall, London. It is September 28, 1988, the night of a concert that seems to celebrate two fantastic years in a new star's career. As yuppies scream "Stevie!" from expensive box seats and young fans run down the aisles to hit a wall of firm but fair bouncers, here is an eighties hero being greeted by his hordes of fresh-faced admirers.

Steve, quietly handsome in a crisp white shirt and fashionable Chinos supported by taut braces, is cool, confident and faintly amused. As he pours his heart and soul into the songs that have endeared him to the CD generation, he glances over at older faces in the audience, people perhaps less willing to shout and scream, but Winwood fans nonetheless.

He purrs through gems from his new album 'Roll With It', 'Don't You Know What The Night Can Do?' and 'Put On Your Dancing Shoes', looks around and says: "Thank you very much, now this is the point in the show when we like to play some of the *older* songs. I think, looking around, that some of you might remember them . . . if you do, let us know!"

Then, the shouting rock anthem 'I'm A Man' swiftly unites all sections of his audience. It was a hit this boyish performer had known the *first* time around, when that other Stevie Winwood of legend was taking his first steps on a road leading him from teenage stardom to hippie dreams, to frustrations and disappointments, to impending obscurity, and finally to the ultimate reward of million-selling hit records, Grammy Awards and the mixture of happiness and respect all artists seek.

The story of Steve Winwood, singer, composer, and multi-instrumentalist is the saga of the last great sixties' rock hero who achieved full fame and recognition . . . just in time.

So many of his talented contemporaries soared and faded while he kept faith with his musical beliefs and adapted his life to suit changing times. An inner strength and determination, perceived through his outward calm and charm, has long held him on the right course, even through the most testing of times.

Steve started his career at such a tender age that even though many of his most loyal fans once feared he might become a lost cause during periods of apparent inactivity, he nevertheless had time to catch up, surpass the efforts of his contemporaries, and still remain younger in years and appearance! Born near Birmingham in 1948, he was a fully-fledged performing artist by the age of 15 and had fully tasted all the rewards and pitfalls of rock stardom before he turned 20.

That night at The Albert Hall was part of a succession of triumphant performances that celebrated not just his return to the spotlight, but many years of major contributions to music. Steve played no less than eight consecutive nights from September 27 to October 6 at the noble Victorian venue, normally the home of classical music and the English equivalent of America's Carnegie Hall.

Together with a 'hometown' show at Birmingham's massive National Exhibition Centre on September 25, the Albert Hall shows climaxed a 1988 'Roll With It' world tour that gave Winwood as much cause for pride and pleasure as his oldest fans. They had seen him develop from a blues singer and guitarist from the English Midlands, into the star of such bands as The Spencer Davis Group, Traffic and Blind Faith, into the mature, sophisticated, but still essentially soulful, performer of the hi-tech eighties. They had seen him too as the shy teenager hitting the London club scene during the peak of the Swinging Sixties, and astounding everyone with a wholly unpretentious and yet supremely confident musical skill. They had witnessed his first round of triumphs, the hit records, the music press headlines and screaming teenage adulation, all of which would come back to him again in the fullness of time.

14

But in between these twin peaks of artistic and commercial success lay years when at times it seemed his artistry might be submerged or the joy of music making lost. There were times when confusion, sadness and illness assailed Winwood. But then came the rewards and pleasures of life due to a man who has given much to music and audiences across the world.

The full flowering of his talents and career in 1988, when he once again stood up, strapped on his guitar and looked and sang at the world boldly in the face, coincided with his own personal maturity and new-found happiness. In the year of his fortieth birthday, memories of the awkward, sometimes scruffy, youth of yesteryear were banished and the tag of reluctant 'Boy Wonder' relegated to myth and legend. Now Steve could truly sing . . . 'I'm A Man'.

Eric Clapton, one of Steve's greatest admirers, sang 'Every-one's Gotta Change' on his 'Money And Cigarettes' album, and this philosophy certainly seemed to be fully accepted by Steve as he moved his career into high gear for the climax of the eighties. As he changed his appearance to become ultra cool, smart and fashionable, so his music reached out to a new, wider audience, and became tougher, closer to rock, soul and his roots. He took steps he would never have contemplated in the laid-back seventies, utilised the power of video, and even agreed to commercial sponsorship.

He played the media game and gave more interviews than at any time in his life, charming writers and reporters with his modesty and sense of humour. The unprecedented exposure allowed a new generation to discover Steve Winwood and his music. The result was huge, world-wide success.

The first signs of Winwood stepping back into the spotlight and the high life came when he toured with his new band for the first time in 10 years in the summer of 1983. Later he appeared on the unique ARMS charity shows held in the autumn of that year.

Maybe he was stung by critics who had described his career as "low key and patchy" or perhaps he sensed that the years were slipping away. At any rate when Steve played the ARMS shows he gave an impressive display of confidence that had not been seen since The Spencer Davis Group days, but had slowly evaporated into self-effacement during his years hiding behind a massive Hammond organ with Traffic.

The concert, again at The Royal Albert Hall, on September 21, 1983 was an emotional event. Ronnie Lane, bass player, writer and singer with The Small Faces, famed for their hits like 'What'cha Gonna Do About It', and 'Lazy Sunday' had sadly contracted the wasting disease of multiple sclerosis.

After three turbulent years with Rod Stewart in The Faces and then forming his own bands, Ronnie was unable to work and had to

15

spend all his money on treatment. Friends rallied round and came up with the idea of all-star charity shows to raise money for Ronnie and for ARMS (Action and Research for Multiple Sclerosis). The Prince and Princess of Wales attended the Royal Albert Hall shows when the bill for any lover of rock music was the ultimate in super-groups. The basic band included chisel-voiced, former Amen Corner singer, Andy Fairweather Low and Rolling Stones Bill Wyman and Charlie Watts, while the main attraction was a guitar front line that featured Jimmy Page, Jeff Beck and Eric Clapton. It was the first time all three ex-Yardbirds guitarists had played 'line abreast', and for many the first important appearance by Jimmy Page since the demise of Led Zeppelin. He celebrated the event by playing a poignant instrumental version of 'Stairway To Heaven'. While the crowds rose to their feet to pay homage to legendary figures back in action, the more discerning noted that the best, most accomplished performance of the night came from a still youthful Steve Winwood, upstaging his elders, just as he had done in the sixties!

His voice rang out, loud, clear and true, with that spine-tingling blues power that is not just 'convincing' but somehow built into him. And he played and played . . . guitar, keyboards, harmonica . . . all the instruments he mastered with such ease in his youth. Steve, surrounded by history makers, still seemed to be the star of the show.

Steve Winwood's solo career, as distinct from his periods with the illustrious groups to whom he lent his talents, began in 1976 when he began recording the 'Steve Winwood' album which was released by Island in June 1977. He worked with a studio band but one of the tracks, 'Midland Maniac', which he wrote, performed, produced and engineered, was completely solo. It was something of a false dawn. Cries of 'patchy' were heard again, then in December 1980, three years later, Island released 'Arc Of A Diver' and the following year it became a big seller, most notably in America. It was his first true solo album but it also marked the beginning of his collaboration with lyricist Will Jennings which continued on to 'Roll With It'.

'Arc Of A Diver' was critically acclaimed and Steve began to think about performing live once again. In 1982 he released 'Talking Back To The Night' and toured Europe and the UK with a six-piece group during 1983. This proved a tremendous success while audiences appreciated his new songs like 'Valerie', released as a single in October 1982, and then re-issued in 1987 when it reached number 19 in the charts.

In July 1985 he began recording in New York City with Russ Titelman as producer. The album they devised was to set the seal on Steve's new success and recognition, and it bore the blatantly up-front and assertive title 'Back In The High Life'. Released in July 1986 it reached number eight in the UK charts and number three in America, earning Steve three Grammy awards and selling over two million copies

STEVE WINWOOD

in the States. Like so many other maturing British rock performers, Steve gained his greatest success and financial rewards in America where his solo career had first taken off with 'Arc Of A Diver'.

The two previous albums were recorded at his home studio, Netherturkdonic, in Gloucestershire and on them he played most of the instruments. In New York he took advantage of the great pool of musical talent available and used a whole range of singers and players, including Chaka Khan, James Ingram, Nile Rodgers and James Taylor. But Steve denied that he brought them together to get a winning formula. He told UK writer Martin Townsend of *Tracks:* "I didn't really get those people in because they were famous. The idea is always to get the best possible sound or approach for the track. For instance I tried out loads of really good bass players. But in the end I played bass myself on some of it because I felt I had the best idea of what I wanted. I didn't particularly want to play bass."

Up to this time it seemed Steve had settled down to country life, going for walks, and playing organ in the local church. Then came the huge success of 'Back In The High Life' which eventually sold four million copies worldwide. Steve told critic Adam Sweeting: "The album gave me a new younger audience in America. It got me out of selling to a faithful few. But I think I also got myself out of it by becoming more accessible."

'Back In The High Life' proved to be Steve's last album made for Island Records, the label founded by Chris Blackwell, who had discovered Steve as a teenager. His departure was a disappointment for Island which was then in the throes of celebrating its 25th anniversary as one of Britain's foremost independent labels. Steve had been managed by Blackwell since 1964, when he was in The Spencer Davis Group, and he began recording for Island in 1967 when Traffic were formed.

Blackwell, who is related to the Crosse and Blackwell family of Jamaican plantation owners, sugar exporters and preserve makers, was one of those key figures in the development of British rock who combined astute business sense with an ear for talent. Like Richard Branson, Chris Blackwell backed his hunches and supported artists, many of whom became major acts. Island proved a welcome home for a rich variety of Jamaican and British artists, including Bob Marley And The Wailers, Free, Roxy Music, Cat Stevens, Robert Palmer, and more recently U2. But even when Winwood's output was down, he appeared to be the jewel in the Island crown as far as the founder was concerned. He was with the label for 20 years, one of the longest such associations in record business annals.

But Steve was determined to 'make changes' and find a better deal. Even the most avuncular managers are not entirely altruistic. Blackwell had built Island on the success of his artists, going right back to

17

The Spencer Davis Group. Now one of his earliest protégés felt it was time to fly the nest and seek more profitable pastures new. The deal offered by Richard Branson's Virgin label was worth a reputed 12 million dollars. It was the first time Steve had received a record company advance.

Said Steve shortly after signing: "When I left Island, it wasn't just that I was keen to leave. I wanted to have a look around and see what other record companies could do for me. I felt Virgin was going to be better for me than Island. It was a bit like changing insurance companies!"

Steve knew that his deal with Island was coming up for renewal and in the past he had always simply re-signed. This time he wanted to check out any alternatives. He examined the workings of different record companies and took the advice of his brother Muff Winwood who proposed that he sign with a major label. "They could get my music heard, which was what I wanted," said Steve. "They can sometimes try and dictate what sort of music you should play but fortunately that didn't happen to me because they were signing an established artist. Richard Branson was looking for something to help him launch in America, where I was strong, and I needed to be stronger in the rest of the world. It seemed better all round. I never decided to leave Blackwell, I thought I'd have a look around to see what else there was and Chris didn't make any better offers. He didn't really have anything to say about it. He left it all up to me. So I presumed he wasn't too interested anyway. We had drifted apart a bit. Also I'd been looking for another manager from the early eighties."

Later, in November 1987, Island would celebrate Steve's years with the company by releasing 'Chronicles', a compilation that featured tracks from each of his four solo albums including the Top Twenty hit 'Valerie', 'Arc Of A Diver' and the majestic 'While You See A Chance'. His first release for Virgin more than repaid the company's faith in him as he unleashed the superb 'Roll With It' in June 1988, a few weeks after the single of the same name and accompanying video. Both album and single went to number one in the US charts, just weeks after release. In fact the album leapt to number six in the US within three weeks of entering the chart. ('Back In The High Life' had taken seven weeks to reach the same position).

The ultra cool LP cover shot of Steve with slicked back hair, black leather jacket and white T-shirt, looking like a more amiable eighties James Dean, was to be seen on a million posters and pieces of merchandise from magazines to tour programmes. History could wait. Here was a *new* star.

The music business welcomed Steve's triumph. In the US, Virgin co-managing director Jeff Ayeroff said ecstatically: "Steve took care of us; we didn't have to take care of him. When we first heard 'Roll

With It' we knew it was a number one record." In fact it was Steve's first number one album in 25 years, and was described by the US rock press as "one of the most important albums of the year."

Showbiz writers trying to explain the Winwood phenomenon described him as "appealing to the same broad-based coalition of pop, rock and adult contemporary fans that has supported such party favourites as Elton John, Billy Joel and Phil Collins."

David Fincher's video for 'Roll With It' was hailed by the music industry as 'the best of the year'. Exclaimed Steve Dupler, writing in *Billboard:* "David Fincher's video for Steve Winwood's new single 'Roll With It' is unquestionably one of the best – if not *the* best clip we've seen this year. Brilliant camera work, a strong symbiosis with the music, and a great overall look combine to make viewing this video a joyous experience."

As usually happens when attention beams down on a particular artist too favourably for too long, there were some niggling voices to be heard. Controversy arose over involvement with Michelob, the beer company who sponsored Winwood's tours. His second single from the album 'Don't You Know What The Night Can Do?' was performed by Steve in a national TV commercial for Michelob and some critics didn't think it right that an artist should stoop to "writing songs for business interests."

Their complaints, however, were based on a misconception, which Winwood is at pains to clear up. Says Steve: "I didn't write the song for Michelob. It was a great song and Michelob came and took it."

In any case, as others were quick to point out, rock has had a long involvement with consumerism, and in recent years sponsorship has helped underwrite the high cost of touring, conversely aiding manufac-turers to reach the vital youth market with their products. Jeff Ayeroff told *Billboard* in August 1988: "It (sponsorship) didn't hurt Eric Clapton, it never hurt Phil Collins. In Japan, where this has been a practice for the last 20 years, everybody from Sting to Bono does commercials. Does the public care? I don't think so, because the public isn't as harsh a critic. Radio runs on familiarity. When a company like Michelob buys $10,000,000 in commercial time, that's $10,000,000 in familiarity."

Steve was quite alarmed and upset by the poor publicity all the controversy created. It seemed to spoil his obvious joy at the great upturn his career had taken, and it all seemed so unnecessary, as he explained to me in May 1989.

"I came in for a lot of bad publicity for doing corporate sponsorship. The way I see it rock journalism in America is now getting like it was in England in 1979. They attach music to political ideology and they say rock 'n' roll shouldn't be involved in corporate sponsorship because it stands for everything that's the opposite to rock's philosophy. That's fine but what is a record company but a corporation?

"For some reason I was caught in the crossfire. I was right in the forefront because of a bit of bad timing by me and my management. What happened was this beer company sponsored the tour which meant they would give us wonderful support and then they'd take one of my songs off the album and make a commercial out of it. That was the deal. But the deal was clinched while I was still working on the album. When it was finished, but before it came out, they took the song they wanted, and very quickly shot the commercial. So what happened was the commercial came out before the album. Then the LP was released and the first single which was 'Roll With It'. Six weeks later the second single was due to be released which was the song they used for the commercial. They started putting the commercial on the TV *before* the single was out. It looked like I had written a beer jingle!"

Steve winces at the memory but is still angry at his treatment. "The major . . . writers . . . for want of a better word . . . the rock intelligentsia did not like that at all, even to the point of lying in the interviews saying: 'Winwood doesn't deny he wrote the song for a beer commercial.' Absolute bloody rubbish! 'Course I didn't write a commercial. I wrote a seven-minute song like I always write. I didn't write a 30-second ditty. They took it and edited it down to a 30-second thing."

But after the accusations of selling out to big business were trumpeted in the rock press, as Steve says: "Every provincial writer in the country then followed suit. It did me a lot of harm really. It did me a lot of damage."

It seemed doubly galling, coming from the land of free enterprise culture where TV sponsorship was invented before Steve was born. "Well that's what I thought. That was my response. I'm getting this thrown at me – in the land of opportunity?"

The damage Steve feared he might have suffered is probably only a storm in a beer can, but he brooded over the injustice and noted that single and album sales fell off in the aftermath. He hopes that by putting the record straight on the way a completely innocuous TV commercial happened to slip out ahead of schedule, his American fans will see that it doesn't mean Winwood has sold his soul to base commercialism.

"When a record does badly, nobody really knows *why*. You can say, 'Oh it was a great album but it wasn't produced properly, or it wasn't promoted properly.' Nobody really knows – or will ever know."

'Roll With It', his début album for Virgin, was as 'stunning' as the record company PRs claimed. For those who had followed Steve's output it was obviously the best produced, most consistent and happiest of albums.

There were eight new songs, seven of them co-written by Steve with Will Jennings. One – 'Hearts On Fire' – was written by Steve with Jim Capaldi, his old drummer mate from Traffic days. The album was produced in Dublin and Toronto by Steve together with Tom Lord Alge, Steve playing most of the instruments, backed by hand-picked sessioneers. These included guitarist Paul Pesco and keyboard players Mike Lawler and Robbie Kilgore.

When the author told Steve that he thought it was the best, most entertaining album he'd ever made, Steve nodded. "Thank you," he said, then added, "well, it was a bit rushed!"

It was felt that simply added to its spontaneity and 'live' feel. "Oh sure. And it sold two million in America, so who can complain. I look upon making albums like making a film. It's an illusion . . . a *delusion!*" he laughs. "Playing live is like theatre. It doesn't mean you can't make great records by setting the band up and playing. You can. But it's not the only way."

21

One of the most significant credits on the album was to his wife Eugenia "for undying support during this project." It was Genia's encouragement that helped Steve take a fresh, firm grip on his career and music.

Steve divorced his first wife Nicole in December 1986. Press reports later claimed that . . . "She had grown accustomed to the country life in the English Cotswolds and Steve felt the call of America where he had to spend more time recording and touring." Alas this interpretation of the rift was far from the truth, as Steve will explain later.

He met and later married his new American lady Eugenia Crafton, a business administration graduate from Tennessee, then aged 27. Eugenia's father was a country doctor and came from a farming background. The wedding took place on January 17, 1987 in New York. Their first child Mary Clare was born in a Nashville hospital on May 20, 1987.

Said Steve: "She loves it in England. And I'm a lot happier now. Everyone tells me that I'm much more settled. Genia has her own career too, in business administration, and she helps check my accounts. In 1986 when there was all the fuss around 'High Life', Genia was doing her exams. I'd be doing a gig and she'd say, 'I hope you don't mind but I've got some work to do.' Then she'd stay in the dressing room while I was on-stage and get the text books out!"

Shortly after they married it was reported they had "bought a ranch" to live on in Tennessee. "That's never been true!" says Steve. "Everywhere I read that I own this ranch, and everyone in Nashville seems to think I own a ranch, but I don't. I don't know where these stories come from."

Steve agrees that his new-found happiness had permeated the music of 'Roll With It'. "I think it's more of a happy album. There's nothing melancholic about it. That's because I'm very, very happy, for several reasons. Firstly at 40-years-old I've had the best album and the best part of my career ever."

True happiness is perhaps best appreciated after having experienced sadness and there have been times of emotional turmoil for Steve, occasioned by the loss of friends like Jimi Hendrix, and Chris Wood of Traffic, and the stress of divorce. Steve has endured the exhaustion of endless touring and the demands of the music business from an early age, he has experienced its fickleness, and the changing of styles and fashions. But throughout it all, he has coped with a disarming resilience, and emerged smiling, armed with the beliefs and advice of his father, that if you had music to fall back on, you'd never be lost or alone.

His childhood environment, family background and the impact of American music all played an important part in his development. Beneath that lay an innate talent, a flair and a feeling that was all his own and has never ceased to amaze and delight those who have grown up, lived and worked with him. Steve has always taken such capabilities in his stride and has never aimed to 'show off' or become a musical egotist. He'll take a quiet pride in his achievements and knows when to put his foot down. He'll take swift, drastic decisions, but always for the best and most practical reasons. Even as a teenager he was nobody's fool.

His story began in Birmingham, England's 'Second City', where he was born in 1948, in the suburb of Handsworth. Next in importance to London, the capital, Birmingham is a centre of manufacturing industry, and rather like Detroit, it has a long history of motor car – and music – making! Birmingham has always had a strong music scene from the days of dance bands and jazz through to the pop and rock eras. It produced many hit groups during the Swinging Sixties, including The Move and The Moody Blues. At a time when English provincial towns were (in the wake of The Beatles' Liverpool break out) gaining their own musical identity and recognition, its best loved band was The Spencer Davis Group. This was the band where, with his older brother Mervyn 'Muff' Winwood, Steve first came to fame and developed his skills.

Originally called The Spencer Davis Rhythm And Blues Quartet, they were Birmingham's first R&B group at a time when English fans were discovering the roots of Black American music, having already assimilated the earlier wave of fifties rock 'n' roll.

Guitarist and folk singer Spencer led the group and brought in drummer Pete York. Together they toured the clubs and won swift acclaim.

They had a string of hits including the Jackie Edwards' song 'Keep On Running' (1965), 'Gimme Some Lovin'' (1966) and 'I'm A

Man' (1967). After their last two hits, which Steve wrote, he left the band to form Traffic and change his musical direction. The Spencer Davis years were fun and crucial to Steve's development. He has fond memories of them, shared by all the band, who frequently get together for private reunions where they can laugh about the 'good old days', although according to Jim Capaldi, his partner in Traffic, Steve finds the sixties "a blur".

Steve agrees and says "The only people who don't remember the sixties are the people who lived through them!"

Some of the clearest recollections of those formative years are held by Muff Winwood, who has developed a key role in the record industry since hanging up his bass guitar and is today head of A&R at CBS Records in London, where he has been responsible for discovering and shaping the careers of many of today's pop stars. The events of the sixties are also still fresh in the memories of Spencer Davis, who now lives in California, drummer Peter York and tour manager John Glover. All shared crucial, life-shaping experiences during one of the most pleasurable periods of Steve's story. However it is to Steve we turn for the greatest insight and perception.

It was the warmest, sunniest day of the year, and the start of a hot summer as the author drove west out of London towards Steve's Gloucestershire home early in May, 1989. It would be pleasant to meet Steve once again. Some years had passed since our last interview at the time of 'Arc Of A Diver'. Much had happened in his life. We had known each other well, particularly in the days of The Spencer Davis Group, and Traffic. In recent years, there had been fewer opportunities to meet and talk but I felt a special pride in seeing success come in such a rush and was profoundly delighted that a great artist was singing, playing and making hit records . . . better than ever.

With Steve jetting around the world, living part of the time in Nashville and forever busy recording, making videos and touring, it is not always easy to track him down. As my car rolled down a winding country road, tapes I'd been playing reached a rousing climax. I'd started out in London with The Spencer Davis Group's first single, 'Dimples' from 1964. Now the cassette player was blasting out the stomping beat of 1988's 'Roll With It', just as the tyres were crunching along the drive leading to a stone built Cotswold manor house set in a hollow that Constable might have painted. All around were trees, sheep and meadows which formed a comforting rural cocoon.

I thought the row I was making as the music blasted through the open sun roof would bring Steve rushing out, but my dramatic arrival petered out as I switched off the tape player, and engine. A silence fell, that great stillness that only the English countryside can produce, even in the age of noise and upheaval. Other counties have been partially destroyed or damaged by motorways and modern farming methods. Gloucestershire seems to have escaped the worst of this fatal impact, something which Steve values highly. As a musician, raised in the city, he more than most, knows the value of peace and tranquility.

Far from being the 'recluse' of press mythology, Steve is open and sociable, enjoys the company of friends and neighbours, and takes special pleasure in the joys of family life. There are some parallels with life in the famed country cottage he shared with Traffic in the sixties. Then he managed to combine home and music-making under one roof. At the house, where he's lived for 20 years, he has much more space for a superbly equipped studio and music room.

Getting out of the car, there didn't seem to be a soul about. Close to the front door there stood a great iron bell handle that didn't look like it had been connected to anything since the corn riots of 1837. I tiptoed into the hall. There came a faint, but instantly recognisable murmur. It was Steve's voice, somehow melodious, warm, strong and positive, tinged with the accents of the industrial Midlands and the American blues heartlands . . . a mixture once heard, never forgotten. His brother Muff sounds very similar, yet neither has the tones of the often parodied 'Brummie' accent.

I decided I couldn't just walk into his house without warning, so I retraced my steps and tried the gnarled handle. A distant bell rang. Steve appeared in the hall. "Come in – we thought you were going to get here earlier!" He'd been waiting for me in the kitchen with Nobby Clark, his trusted aide and tour manager for many years.

Later I was introduced to Steve's wife Eugenia and their daughter Mary Clare. She stared at me with grave suspicion, then pushed a ball in my direction. I threw it back expecting her to catch it. I'd forgotten that little girls don't indulge in such undignified games, especially with new visitors. She eyed me with a solemn gaze, then smiled.

"Would you like some tea?" asked Steve and soon we were relaxed in the kitchen where a large black Aga stove simmered. Eugenia had to go out and the rest of the household too had their chores to attend to and visits to make. Soon Steve and I were alone in the house, apart from, as I discovered later, Tom Lord Alge, the American engineer, who was staying at the house and was busy in the nearby studio.

Clad in blue jeans and a check shirt, Steve looked much the same as I remembered him, older of course, but still slim and boyish, even at 40. Above all he was wonderfully patient with my requests to talk about his career, coping with old issues and long-forgotten controversies. He seemed most animated and at ease talking about either his childhood or recent exploits which represented the happiest times. Talk of eras in between occasionally drew a distant response when I couldn't be sure if he simply didn't want to remember something, or his memory had indeed faded. And then he surprised me by grasping the nettle and explaining frankly something about himself and his character during the earliest periods of his musical career that was strongly self-critical.

I felt he was being harsh on his younger self. Whatever changes he has undergone, Steve today is a man largely at peace, contented, occasionally alarmed or dismayed by things he sees going on around him, exasperated by media misinterpretation, but generally feeling as fulfilled as most men have a right to be after years of work and achievement.

While Steve Winwood is charming, eloquent and courteous, he still has that impish smile of a natural musician who can recognise bull and baloney when he hears it and slide in a sharp or pithy observation about someone or something when roused. During our conversation he railed about a number of issues, from the destruction of Birmingham city centre to the misuse of modern symphony orchestras. But what bothers him most is being the object of distorted stories. "That's a great book – if you like fiction," he said, pointing to a biography of Steve Winwood lying on a table in his lounge.

This was the scene for a conversation that would range over his earliest childhood memories, his discovery of music, development of his instrumental ability, the acquisition of a unique singing voice, and his school days. Then came his first experiences in bands, the rise of The Spencer Davis Group, subsequent developments with Traffic, Blind Faith, Airforce, his session work and the evolution of his solo career, culminating in his current enormous success.

His memories and comments are interspersed through the following narrative, combined with the recollections of colleagues and contemporary reports, many of them from our past interviews which first appeared in the sixties. Steve seemed pleased, and often amused to be reminded of gigs he'd long forgotten. He was amazed to hear Traffic had played on pop 'package' shows and couldn't believe they'd shared a bill with Vanilla Fudge.

Steve sat on a sofa opposite me in the large room whose main feature was a huge ingle-nook stone fireplace. This was no up-market executive show-house style 'extra' though – this was the real thing. "This house would have belonged to a weaver, and as he grew richer, so he would have added larger rooms," explained Steve.

Several such houses were built by farmers who had grown rich on the profitable Cotswold wool trade around 1500. "This house wasn't built all at the same time. The owners would add an extra piece on when they were doing well. From the outside you can see that it was originally a cottage. There was a house here from Norman times and it's mentioned in the Domesday book. Most of it was built in the 16th and 17th centuries while the outhouses were built in the 19th."

Later we adjourned to the studio where Tom Alge was busy working on a video and sound recording of Winwood's shows at The Royal Albert Hall due for showing on US cable TV and to be made available as a commercial video. Tom showed us the video, which Steve watched carefully to make sure the live action was in sync with the soundtrack. Just then Tom said quietly to Steve: "There's a guy walking up the path. Do you know him?" Suddenly I thought how vulnerable we were out in the country. The intruder, bold as brass walked straight into the studio.

"I'm looking for Steve Winwood," he announced, looking at Steve as he spoke. The object of his search smiled and said diffidently, "Well, you've found him, that's me." It transpired the uninvited guest was a lyricist who needed a songwriter and he'd been told this guy Winwood was something to do with the music business. He had a curt, abrupt, fussy manner that left us taken aback. He complained that he'd already made three previous visits and phone calls and that Steve had always been out. Now he had hired a car specially to come down for this visit, and expected this Winwood fellow to come up with some material. As I had been waiting for a chance to talk to Steve for two years, I felt like strangling the man who was wasting precious minutes. Mercifully Steve took charge by gently leading him out of the studio into the house, treating him with a respect he didn't deserve. Incredibly, after Steve had made the suggestion that he leave a tape of his material, this would-be co-writer protested loudly that he couldn't possibly leave a tape if he couldn't be sure he'd get it back again. Steve told us later he offered to give him a pound for the postage. And he was still grumbling and complaining.

"We get these sort of people all the time," revealed Tom. "Normally we keep a look out."

"It's ever since the papers printed my address," said Steve with a rueful smile. "Nice of them. It's a wonder they didn't give the zip code as well."

We went for a wander round the outhouses. There was the 'dinosaur' room, not filled with the mouldering bones of old groups, but equipment, including a grand piano that was now redundant. "It's all done by sampling now," said Steve. "I used to have a pipe organ – but who needs a pipe organ, or a grand piano when you can get the same effect by sampling?"

Steve had planned lunch in the local pub, The Plough, but by the time we got around to calling them, the pub had closed, and we drove into the village instead. We bought some cling wrapped cheese and ham and a loaf and came home to the deserted manor house, where Steve prepared tea. He is planning to experiment with home beer brewing (as an alternative to certain brands he cheerfully describes as "gnats piss"), but sadly hadn't had time to prepare any. We talked in the kitchen, and then out in the garden in the hot sun. During the afternoon I became vaguely aware that, even in the depths of the English countryside that Steve loves so well, the silence can be disturbed by the distant roar of agricultural machinery and thunder of jets heading west to America.

Even so there is a calm in Gloucestershire that permeates Winwood too, and makes him the most restful and relaxing company. His sense of humour surfaces in a disarming way, and he laughs often, even at the greatest blunders perpetrated by those who would tell the story of his life, including myself.

"You see," he would say from time to time, "they've got it *all* wrong."

Let's hope from here on we get it right.

27

the kid can play!

Lawrence and Lillian Winwood lived with their two sons, Mervyn (nicknamed Muff) and Stephen in a small but comfortable terraced house at Atlantic Road, in Kingstanding, Birmingham. The couple were married just before the start of World War II. Muff was born on June 15, 1943, and Steve was born just over five years later on May 12, 1948, in a Handsworth nursing home and not in the house of a relative as has been claimed elsewhere. "It wasn't a house. I wasn't born in anybody's home. That's a great fiction. Where on earth people get that stuff from I've no idea," says Steve.

Lawrence Winwood was works manager at a West Midlands engineering company and was also a keen amateur musician. During the war he worked with the design team that produced the Norton 500 motorcycle. Later he was employed by Steve's great uncle who had a foundry in Smethwick called Hall Foundries. He was general manager until he retired 15 years ago.

"Just a couple of years after he left the whole place folded," says Steve. "He didn't believe in management schools. He thought the personal touch was best and in my opinion he had a fantastic relationship with the shop floor because he would just work with them and never set himself apart in any way. The staff all thought he was great. They churned out metal goods like washers and stuff, and it was one of those typical Victorian Black Country factories that you see the remains of today. After the seventies recession it all went. All the while he was working there he was playing in bands. He played sax and clarinet, but he played other instruments and did gigs as a bass player too, and on the drums. If he could get a gig as a drummer he'd go and do it."

An upright piano stood in the lounge at home and there was always music in the Winwood household. There was even a drum kit in the garage and a double bass. As a child Steve would explore all these instruments and enjoyed "bashing away" on the drum kit. "I was very interested in music too but Steve got to grips with the piano whereas I couldn't," says Muff. "Although Dad was a tenor sax player I still couldn't learn how to tongue the clarinet properly, and couldn't get going on piano lessons. So I hit a problem that I couldn't express. Steve, who was five years younger, was lifted on to the piano stool and found a way in straight away. He just started to play."

One of his first pieces was the National Anthem, but Muff and his parents were amazed to find that Steve could play any little tune they whistled. The Winwood parents both came from large families. Their mother had eight brothers and their father had seven brothers and in both families every single member was a musician. Recalls Muff: "They were either a church organist, a violinist in the local orchestra, a brass player in an army band and out of all of those uncles and aunts from both sides of the family, they all had children and not one of them had music passed down to them. I think the whole of the musical talent of both sides of the family fell on Steve. Among his cousins, both male and female . . . few of them have any particular musical interest at all."

Steve remembers: "There were always banjos and mandolins knocking around when I grew up, and the piano, so I had plenty of opportunity. I wasn't forced into music, I was gently encouraged, so I was lucky. My mother's father was also a musician. He was a church organist and he played the fiddle. He was a Welshman and they say I take after him. The instruments I had, I really abused.

"There was one instrument – a beautiful thing I wish I still had. It was a banjo version of a tenor mandolin with four double strings and tuned in fifths. And I remember . . . I played cricket with it, and ruined it! Although I showed some interest, I didn't get seriously into music until six when I started to pick out a tune on the piano."

A great uncle's son, Steve's second cousin, played a baby grand piano and he also had a mini-piano, an over-strung instrument, somewhat fashionable in the fifties. "I think my dad sprayed his car for him and for that we got the piano! Our old piano by then was in pretty bad shape."

Among the elders there were many musical evenings when the family members played their set pieces. Steve: "We used to go round to my grandmother's. She played the piano and the only song I remember her playing was 'Little Brown Jug'. She could play quite well. It was in the days before the telly. It sounds terrible when you say things like this but I actually remember us being one of the first people in the street that had a TV. Neighbours would come round to watch it. I told Genia that when I was young they used to deliver milk on a horse and cart. And she said: 'I wouldn't tell too many people that!' But they did – and the bread."

Both brothers would play and all the family would sing. One played a one-string fiddle with a horn on it. In fact right up until their mother died in 1988 they would still get together at Christmas at Muff's home and sing carols.

Says Steve: "We'd get round the piano and Muff would play the guitar and lead everyone and call out 'All the women sing this bit,' and conduct everyone. Dad gave up playing when he retired and sold all his instruments. Of course a few years later he missed them, so we got together and bought him some new ones. He just plays for his own enjoyment now."

Spencer Davis too remembers the Winwoods were famous for their musical evenings. "When there was a wedding or a birthday all the Winwood family got together and somebody would play sax, trumpet or piano. The whole family could put a band together."

Steve: "Although I wouldn't say we were brought up in a great folk tradition, it was certainly nice to be part of the era of making music at home."

At that age Winwood had no thoughts about becoming a professional musician although he swiftly realised he had developed a special skill.

"But it didn't mean any more than being able to do something like . . . bend your thumbs back . . . do you know what I mean? It just seemed like a trick really. At that age I never thought seriously about it. It was like playing marbles or having a good conker!"

Music then, was a facet of childhood, a hobby or pastime, like football. But as his ability was recognised, naturally his dad was keen to offer encouragement.

When Steve showed more interest in piano his father organised lessons which he didn't much enjoy. Steve liked to play by ear and didn't take to the discipline of learning how to read music. The teacher would try to explain how a piece of music went by singing the phrases, and his pupil would immediately play it – but without reading, only by ear. This was only revealed when the teacher asked him to play another piece, without first singing the melody. Muff: "Of course, Steve couldn't play it at all. He was caught out. His reading was never good and he lost interest in learning."

Says Steve: "I remember . . . they took me to a little man down the road. Actually I shouldn't say little man – he was quite a big bloke really. His name was Mr Waldron. He taught me to read, and I learned to play simple pieces by Hoffmann, 'Teddy Bears' Picnic' was one tune I remember. I used to cheat really badly because at the time I was too lazy to learn to read notation properly, and it was much easier just to listen and copy and play by ear. He would sit down and play something, then I'd sit down and play the first few lines just like he'd played it, but I wasn't really reading."

The tutor thought this impressive but confided to Steve's parents there really wasn't anything he could do with him.

Steve went to Cranbourne Road primary school in Kingstanding and he vaguely remembers playing solo piano there at a concert while other boys played clarinet and accordion. "But I wasn't really involved in music much at the primary school. And because Muff was five years older than me I never really saw him much at either school. When I went on to the comprehensive, he had just left. I was 11 and he was 16. I first got a guitar, when I was about nine." But he had already begun fooling around on his brother's guitar – and not always to Muff's great delight.

"Muff and I used to play music together, especially when we both had guitars. He got his before me. First he started to play clarinet because my dad always said if you want to play the sax then you've got to play the clarinet first. I could never handle it, and Muff tried but when he realised he couldn't do that he got a guitar. And of course when he got one, I immediately wanted one. I said 'How come he gets a guitar and I don't.' So I got an acoustic – with metal strings. Later we would play together. He would play the rhythm stuff and I'd play the solos."

Muff agrees: "When I first had the guitar, I had trouble playing solo lines." But he hadn't taken up the guitar just as another hobby. It was all part of a wider, burgeoning social change.

In the early fifties British pop music was thriving well enough but in a way that would be quite baffling to today's music audience. It was the age of big bands, 78 rpm acetate discs which broke if you dropped them on the floor, rationed pop on BBC radio's Light Programme and a network of ballrooms where dance bands would play beneath spinning silver balls which reflected beams of light on to the dancers below. There were hit records, but these consisted entirely of romantic ballads, bright novelties and songs from American shows and movies. For the more daring and bohemian elements there was modern and traditional jazz.

"Dennis Lotis and Lita Rosa were high in the charts then," says Muff. "Then rock 'n' roll started to come in. I realised that I could unleash some of my musical fantasies through the guitar, so my dad bought me the guitar and I remember toiling away at the chord shapes. I got all that together quite well and was soon accompanying Steve when he played the hits by Russ Conway and Winifred Atwell, who were big piano players of the day. Steve was fantastic at that, playing two-handed stuff at the age of six. He was great at parties. I picked up guitar at the same time."

One day Muff was shattered by an experience that could have destroyed his ego for all time. "Steve was about seven I think when he picked up my guitar and said: 'All you have to do is *this*.' And started playing. I thought, this is *ridiculous*. I remember throwing it down and saying to my mum, 'I'm not going to play, it's a waste of time. Every time I try to play anything he just picks it up and does it a hundred times better. What chance have I got?' In many ways I felt this pressure on me all my life. I may well have stayed a professional musician a lot longer than I did, but when you are under the shadow like that, it actually cramps your style. Even when I was in our group together later, I found after switching from guitar to bass Steve could still take my instrument away from me and do it better, instantly. It was forever like banging your head against a brick wall. So when Steve eventually left The Spencer Davis Group to join Traffic I decided to give up playing in a band and get out into the record business . . .!"

Muff makes his complaints without rancour or a sense of griping. In fact he was always immensely proud of his brother's achievements, even if it was hard to live with, especially as a kid with his own ambitions to consider.

"Oh yeah, sure I am proud. I am knocked out for Steve. He does great. But that is how he started and he really had such a quick ear despite the fact that learning to read was a chore. When Steve picked up the guitar and showed me how I was supposed to do it, I got my father to get Steve a guitar as well because The Shadows had started to come in and if he could play lead lines like that we could have a group together."

The cosy age of the crooners and big bands was abruptly shattered by the impact of American rock 'n' roll on British youth. It is an event that has been documented many times, but only those who lived through it will readily appreciate the excitement it aroused. A whole generation became immersed in the hits of Elvis Presley, Bill Haley, Fats Domino, Jerry Lee Lewis and Little Richard, and thousands of bequiffed teenagers were encouraged to start playing themselves. Those who had made their own acoustic guitars in woodwork lessons, to join in the skiffle craze, now took advantage of relaxed hire purchase conditions to buy their first electric guitars and amplifiers. The seeds for the development of British rock were sown.

It was Lonnie Donegan's skiffle hit 'Rock Island Line' in 1956 that single-handedly sparked the home-made music boom among young British teenagers. It resulted in a vast outpouring of amateur guitarists who were soon to turn to playing electric rock, or blues guitar. Donegan introduced the blues into pop music.

"We were interested in skiffle because it was very much a home-based thing," says Muff. "You could knock up a skiffle group in no time at all and the music really was a mix of black blues and white country. This led us into finding out more about the blues.

"I also played Steve all my early rock 'n' roll records and later stuff I picked up at the youth club like the Isley Brothers' 'Twist And Shout'. Steve specially liked Fats Domino, but we got into Cliff Richard and The Shadows because it was easy to play their numbers. Steve could play the lead lines and I was good at all the chords."

Although it has been suggested that Lawrence Winwood had a huge collection of jazz records with which he was supposed to have indoctrinated his children, Steve remembers things rather differently: "In fact," he says with a smile, "to tell you the truth I never *had* a record player. I got one later on. My dad's oldest brother who is still alive, is an extraordinary chap. He used to make things – like his own refrigerator. He built a fantastic model railway, and he had a beautiful garden. He'd do his own photography and developing and built his own hi-fi systems, completely from scratch. And he also built a tape recorder. After he finished making these things, he'd never sell them. That would spoil things for him, if it became a business. He used to make his own clothes as well. As kids we used to love to go round there and play with the trains."

After he'd made the tape recorder he wanted to make an even better one, so the Winwoods were given the old model. Steve and Muff got hold of an FM radio tuner and recorded all their favourite music off the radio. "Highly illegal!" laughs Steve. "But that's how we heard our music. We used to listen to rock 'n' roll on Radio Luxembourg. It wasn't until much later that we actually got a record player. I remember another cousin had a wind up gramophone and he had a 78 rpm record of Elvis Presley's 'Hound Dog' which was fantastic. We just kept playing that. And I never actually owned the record. My dad liked Dixieland jazz and Muff liked more modern jazz but there wasn't such a distinction then. My dad used to listen to Simon Phillips' dad's band, who was Sid Phillips the clarinet player. He thought that was a great band and so we used to listen to that."

Playing with local dance bands in the evenings and at wedding receptions, Lawrence Winwood was plagued with requests for modern rock melodies which were difficult to play with a sax and trumpet front line. He said to his boys: "Why don't you come along and in the middle of the set do The Shadows numbers with our bass player and drummer?" So Steve and Muff had their first professional playing experience working clubs, private functions and weddings with their dad's band.

"In those days you didn't have a disco," says Muff. "They weren't invented. You had dance bands with a couple of saxes and rhythm. I used to play all the way through with the band on guitar, and Steve had to be locked away in a room behind the band because he was too young to be in these licensed premises. He was wearing short trousers and kept hidden. Then after they had half a dozen requests to play the latest Elvis Presley hit or whatever, Steve would be called on . . . and we used to go down a storm."

Muff is still amazed at the memory of those early gigs in smoke-filled rooms. "We used to play 'Red River Rock' by Johnny And The Hurricanes and I got my dad to play, very badly, the chicken clucking sax solo, and hits by The Shadows and Duane Eddy. Steve and I worked out half a dozen numbers, and they wouldn't let us leave! And of course there weren't many bands about doing this, it was very new. If you were driving along the street and saw a kid walking along with a guitar in his hands you would screech to a halt and say, 'Excuse me, what's your name, where do you live, can we phone you up?' Now kids walking around with a guitar are 10 a penny, but then in Birmingham in the early fifties it was a rarity."

35

Guitars were expensive and parents had to be very keen on music to be cajoled into forking out the money that might otherwise be earmarked for a new TV set or washing machine. Most teenagers then couldn't afford a guitar so the Winwood brothers were considered rather special in their local area. Muff organised the school bands and he found he could get into any band he wanted by promising that he had a brother who could play keyboards, guitar or anything. "I could always be in the band because I could bring Steve!"

Steve also remembers those early gigs with his dad. "Yeah . . . we used to sit down and play. We did Shadows songs and they all loved that, but we also did the standards, quicksteps and foxtrots. We played at weddings and big works' dances. That was around 1958. I do remember going to see Cliff Richard and The Shadows at one of their earliest shows around that time."

Before they got into home-grown British rock hits by Cliff Richard and The Shadows, they had a strong interest in jazz of all types, particularly the guitar playing of Django Reinhardt. Says Steve: "As well as Django we also liked the English player who did that style, Diz Disley. It must be great to be entrenched in one style, but I never really was. I never picked one niche and said 'Okay, I'm just gonna be a blues drummer.' I never did that. I always wanted to play a bit of blues, a bit of piano, some rock 'n' roll on the guitar!"

A big influence on British youngsters brought up during the late fifties was the documentary movie *Jazz On A Summer's Day* which, on release in 1959, introduced a huge range of music to receptive ears.

From the introspective clarinet playing of Jimmy Guiffre on his delicately funky 'Train And The River' to a rare early glimpse of Chuck Berry unleashing Memphis-style R&B, the film was packed with delights and proved a surprise hit at the box office.

"I was 11 when the film came out," says Steve. "It opened a whole Pandora's Box of music for me. Actually I never got to see the movie when it first came out, because I was too young to go, but I heard a lot of the soundtrack. I just liked the way the film brought together so many different elements, from blues to modern jazz.

"But there were other things that affected us too, from Buddy Holly to skiffle. Muff and I played a lot of skiffle stuff, but we didn't form a serious skiffle group as such. Since I've been spending time in Nashville I have realised that the majority of the skiffle songs I heard as a kid were all bluegrass songs. They were the songs I played with Muff that we first heard on *Saturday Club* on BBC Radio on Saturday mornings with DJ Brian Matthews. We used to record them and learn the songs!"

While in Nashville Steve and Genia often visit a sparsely attended bluegrass club that has become something of a mecca for Steve. "There's hardly anybody there but all these great blokes come down and play these old songs, and most of them I know. From skiffle I went on to Django Reinhardt and little bits of jazz. I got into modern jazz after *Jazz On A Summer's Day*. By that time I had left primary at the age of 11 and gone on to comprehensive school."

Steve and Muff both went to Great Barr, one of the first comprehensives in Britain to replace the former Grammar school system and bring the benefits of a broader secondary education to all. "I was a guinea pig pupil and Steve was five years behind me," says Muff. "The new system was a big change for the country, like the coming of the M1 Motorway."

In the same year as Muff was Martin Shaw, the actor who came to fame in TV's *The Professionals*. When Steve arrived at the school he mixed well enough with his fellow pupils and got on well with lessons. He was good at maths, but there was no real encouragement as far as his musical ability was concerned, at least not from the headmaster. One of the teachers organised a guitar club and later, in 1961 Steve attended Birmingham's Midlands Institute for piano lessons, where he studied classical music for a while.

"I wasn't there for more than a year. It didn't work out great . . . it worked out terribly really!" Steve admits his teacher John Rust didn't have an easy time with young Winwood. "I just didn't have the discipline you need to be a classical pianist. The first thing he told me was you can't be a guitarist – and a pianist. That kinda got me the wrong way, y'know. He told me I'd lose sensitivity in my left hand and I'm sure that's right for a certain kind of piano playing but not for the kind of playing I wanted to do . . . Jerry Lee Lewis! Callouses on the left hand would be perfect for that! So that didn't go down too well. But I learnt to read music in stages and also at school during 1959 to '60 I learnt classical guitar as well. I never got on too well with that either. I didn't get as far as Segovia but it was pretty tough. I had to play scales and of course they are terribly hard. I've never been a great practiser. I'd spend hours playing but not practising as such. That's why these teachers had such a hard time with me."

Steve rated himself then as an "average pupil". He'd do his practice routines but would be far happier playing new chords and inversions. It wasn't until years later when he started playing the organ in his local village church in Berkshire that he began to find sight reading from sheet music came to him more easily.

"All that came into play and it was a great discipline. There were four or more lines to play at once including the pedals.

"I did have trouble sight reading at first. They had a pre-war Hammond organ which had all the church pre-sets on it, a fantastic old thing, with a full pedal board. It used to crackle and pop. All the rubber wiring was eaten by mice and stuff and there were insects nibbling away at it!"

When Steve was at the Midland Institute he discovered classical music for the first time. He was actually a part-time student at the Institute while going to Great Barr comprehensive. "They accepted me because I guess they thought I had some ability but it didn't fit in with what they expected. Eventually the crunch came when I admitted I played rock 'n' roll and jazz with some people and they said I couldn't do both. They just lost interest in me."

Music teaching was still a strict Victorian affair in the early sixties but attitudes have changed since and it is unlikely a budding Steve Winwood today would receive such cold rejection simply because he wanted to play modern styles. In fact at today's comprehensive schools where music is taught, jazz and rock music are part of the curriculum, especially in America. "Today's teachers help pupils form rock bands at school, but there was no encouragement then," says Steve.

Of his school days, Muff believes: "He didn't have any special music lessons. In those days, the large comprehensive school system hadn't got itself together. It didn't give any more music lessons than the average kid got, like the life story of Mozart . . . that type of stuff. He sang in the choir but didn't do any playing at school at all. He and I were in the Wolf Cubs, and were involved in the pantomimes. I used to play the ukulele and he used to play the piano. I don't remember him playing at school but by the time he had settled in there, at the age of 13 he was starting to gig around. The headmaster didn't approve of that at all and the biggest problem was he would fall asleep in the lunch hour! He'd often fall asleep in lessons, because he'd been working the night before."

Steve remembers Muff having a school band at Great Barr Comprehensive when he (Steve) was 12. They used to rent the school hall and play. The personnel varied. "Some of the guys really knew about the blues, and we started playing gigs at colleges. The first gig I remember playing to an audience was with Muff's band at a community centre dance. I was on piano and Muff was playing guitar."

Steve did have one music teacher at Great Barr who helped him a lot. "I was lucky enough to have a great music teacher there. Mr Fanshaw was a fantastic chap, he really was. He was really encouraging and did what he could. He let me and another kid who played bass guitar go down to the music hut to play and listen to records."

For years Steve played around in pubs and clubs. Muff had his own outfit The Muff Woody Jazz Band which played Dixieland and mainstream. Steve was the piano player, and the upright pianos they used were always turned with the bulk of the instrument facing the audience, so nobody in authority could spot an underage pianist!

"He could have been kicked out," says Muff. "He sat behind the piano and if you were out on the dance floor you couldn't see it was a kid playing. It was the only way we could get him to be our pianist in the jazz band. We did all these things side by side. There was no chronological order to events. After we started to play in my father's dance bands we moved to Shadows-type local groups at school, and I got the jazz thing together at the same time. We were doing all three things at once, probably enough to keep us working three nights a week."

Muff had by now left school and Steve, by the age of 13, was out playing several nights a week when he should have been studying for his GCE. "He was on a deep downward spiral as far as his schoolwork was concerned. Our parents knew he was alright with his older brother, and my father felt that you couldn't stop it. He felt that after having come through the war years and the workless thirties before that, the ability to play a musical instrument meant you would never starve. It was a thirties attitude. Nobody would ever say that now to their child, because our lives are so different. But he felt if you could play you could sit on a street corner and collect money. You could always entertain for money somewhere. With that kind of attitude my father always had, he didn't want to stop Steve. Certainly he could see what a good player he was and encouraged him as much as possible. He certainly encouraged him to play at weekends, although he wasn't too sure about mid-week gigs!"

There was always a problem about getting Steve up in the morning for school but the pattern of his future life as a professional musician was already set. Meanwhile rock 'n' roll, far from being the passing fad some had predicted, was changing, producing new styles and artists and sustaining its grip on the imagination.

Rock 'n' roll brought a major technical change to pop music. The forties saw the introduction of the electric guitar, with Charlie Christian developing jazz guitar and Les Paul pioneering multi-tracking. In the late fifties American musicians realised that a small group armed with electric instruments could fill a ballroom. Says Muff: "Fifteen musicians used to have to fill it before. Now they could split the money four ways instead of 15. These are the things that really inspired the great changes in musical history. People caught on that the quicker you could amplify yourself the quicker you could produce a smaller group that earned more money. That was all part of the crossover from the dance band era to the rock era. There was a lot of traditional jazz in the UK at the time that was part of the dance music scene too.

"Through skiffle, jazz and rock we started to realise there was a root to all this which was in the blues. The first thing that Steve and I heard that really turned our heads was Ray Charles' 'What'd I Say'. This and 'Hit The Road Jack' were both pop hits in the UK and that was the first time we heard a rock musician crossing over into a jazz form. There was more to Ray Charles than there was to Chuck Berry or Little Richard. He had a deeper, rootsier sound that you couldn't quite put your finger on."

The discovery of Ray Charles, the brilliant soul and gospel singer and pianist, by the Winwood brothers coincided with the period when Steve's voice began to break. "He was 13 when his voice broke," says Muff. "Up until then he had never sung a note. Well . . . we were in the church choir together, and did weddings on Saturday afternoons, and gigs at night . . . but he didn't sing in our groups. As his voice broke, he heard Ray Charles and he used to sit at the church organ after the weddings had finished. In those days you couldn't go to a local music shop and buy an organ. They were only to be found in churches."

Just like so many of the original black soul artists, Steve's earliest singing experiences were on sanctified ground. When the church organist had finished playing, taken his cassock off and got on his bicycle to go home, Steve and Muff used to stay in the church with a couple of other friends, switch on the pump and get the organ going. With Steve pedalling furiously he sang out 'What'd I Say' his voice echoing to the rafters of St. Johns, Perry Bar, in North Birmingham. The Vicar of St. Johns, who was also the Winwoods' choir master, is now the Canon of Birmingham and in December 1987 he visited Steve's house to christen his baby daughter.

"We kept that family link for years," says Muff. "Steve sang in the choir because he had that Aled Jones type voice."

"Not quite!" says Steve. Aled Jones was one of Britain's most celebrated choir boys, gifted with a wonderful treble voice. "I think I had a fairly unremarkable voice. I could hold a tune but I wasn't an outstanding singer in the church choir. There was no real quality in my voice at the time."

Muff used the Aled comparison to emphasise that his brother didn't have a deep baritone voice. "When his voice broke, just at the time he first heard Ray Charles, I think it made a very significant difference to how his career went. As his voice was breaking he kind of moulded it to sound like Ray Charles. While most people's voices break naturally, he forced his voice to sound like Ray and the moment it had finally broken it became *natural*, with a deepness and raspy sound that no other kid had got. If he had discovered Ray Charles two years later his voice may never have been what it is today. But as his voice changed from a child's to a man's, suddenly, overnight he became a singer!"

Steve still speaks with awe about the impact hearing Ray Charles had on him. "It was around 1962. I never saw him play live but I thought the LP 'Ray Charles In Person' recorded live in Atlanta, was the most fantastic record I'd ever heard. Most of the records I've ever had have gone over the years, but miraculously I managed to hold on to a copy of that. It was terribly scratched." When Steve was in LA for the Grammy Awards in 1988, he met a representative of Atlantic Records and asked if he could get a DAT copy of the Ray Charles' classic. "I never thought any more about it. Then it arrived in the post! It was on a remastered Compact Disc. They'd put it together with some other extraordinary Ray Charles' stuff I'd never heard before."

Although Steve was blown away at an early age by Charles' records, Ray wasn't the only influence, and whereas the music scene would abound with imitators, Steve's voice somehow seemed the most authentic, least affected or stylised. Like his absorption of jazz piano styles, where he got the timing and feel right, so his singing had an instantly acceptable maturity, and an unmistakably Winwoodian inflection and sound.

"The thing was I'd always been interested in jazz, blues, rock 'n' roll and skiffle, and suddenly here was this man who in some way, combined all those elements. Yeah! He was fantastic!" Through all his career Steve never actually met Ray Charles, but it was something he always hoped would happen.

Now, not only was Steve playing lead guitar or piano in their various groups, he now became the vocalist. Muff's band had been playing traditional jazz, à la Chris Barber and Alex Welsh, with Steve plonking away on the piano four to the bar, but now they began to unleash their newly acquired repertoire of Ray Charles' hits, with a funky authenticity that was astounding, at least to anyone with half an ear for roots music. At that time, even in Birmingham, the second largest city in Britain, there was only one record shop that specialised in imported blues, jazz and soul. Liverpool, being a port, got a better deal, with merchant seamen (so the story goes) bringing in American records which fuelled Merseybeat and The Beatles.

"That was all going on unbeknown to us in Birmingham," says Muff. "Nobody knew about The Beatles, and you couldn't really get rhythm and blues records except at one shop called The Diskery which was in Broad Street, Birmingham. We eventually got to know the guy who ran the place and he used to let Steve and I flick through thousands of imports and find Big Bill Broonzy and stuff. We discovered the great Black American musical heritage."

"I guess it was around '62 that I started singing in groups," says Steve. "My voice broke at the same time when I was 13." In fact he had been vocalising before that age in the church choir. Although he hadn't been singing the kind of music that would make him famous, he feels it was an important part of his later development. "What I used to sing in the church choir really had a great influence on me, and it influenced me in Traffic and in the stuff I do now, on songs like 'When You See A Chance Take It'. It's easy to say Ray Charles was an influence on me, but I also listened to Wesleyan hymns, and I liked the chord changes and psalm melodies. I suppose that did really have an effect on me. I sang in the choir from the age of seven to 13. The hymns I learned were beautiful."

The Winwoods' jazz band was invited to play at a Sunday morning pub gig where all the Birmingham musicians met to have a blow. Word had spread that Muff's outfit featured a great little player and they couldn't wait to see him in action. Their set was a big success and afterwards the local musos crowded around to congratulate Steve on his performance.

One of them was a student from Birmingham University called Spencer Davis and another was a drummer called Pete York who played in a jazz group. Spencer approached Steve and said: "Hey, you're singing Ray Charles! I'm a folk singer, but I like to sing the blues as well. Why don't we get a little group together? With your jazz blues and my folk blues, we could put them together and make a blues group. We could play every week at the University doing that."

Steve and Muff both thought it was a great idea. The Spencer Davis Group was born.

here we go again!

Spencer David Nelson Davis was born in Swansea in South
Wales on July 17, 1942. A charming, enthusiastic and educated
man, he was to play an important role in Steve's career, both as mentor
and as the man who provided a steady framework in which to develop as
an artist. Steve would eventually outshine his senior partner, as he did
most of the musicians he worked with over the years, but long after their
careers diverged, Steve never forgot his happy and successful Spencer
days. At the time there was much hard work, and strain, as the schoolboy
turned pro musician became a pop star. The pressures of success placed a
burden on all of them but at their peak, The Spencer Davis Group was a
comradely and much-loved band. Not only their fans, but those around
them felt affection for the 'Spencers'. That was unique on a scene noted
for some pretty tough and unlovable characters.

Spencer went to Grammar school in Swansea where he was a
very bright pupil. He seemed destined to be a teacher, but his first job,
taken out of desperation, was as a clerk in a Customs and Excise office.
Returning to the student life, he became fluent in German, and gained
degrees in Modern Languages from both Birmingham and West Berlin

Universities. He also learned to speak French and Spanish, and during the seventies when he temporarily retired from the music scene he used his linguistic skills as a technical translator in the aviation and mining industries. But his first love has always been folk music, the blues and rock 'n' roll, and from an early age he developed his prowess as a singer, guitarist and composer.

Says Spencer: "My grandfather played trumpet and my uncle Leslie played the banjo so I had instruments around me from the earliest days, and I'd wanted a guitar ever since I was a kid," he says. He made his first record when he was 16, a 78 rpm version of Buddy Holly's 'Oh Boy' with 'Midnight Special' on the B-side.

He remembers first meeting Steve Winwood when he was at Birmingham University in 1962. "I used to sing in the London folk clubs and in a jazz band at the university. I went to a pub called The Golden Eagle to see a band called The Renegades. I lugged my 12-string guitar along and a beaten up amplifier and harmonica around my neck held up with coat hanger wire and did a couple of blues and a Leadbelly tune. Then I went into 'Got My Mojo Working' which was the national anthem of the whole R&B movement. If you played that the promoters would say, 'Can you come back next week?'

"If you've ever been in a room where one era of music has been replaced by another, so clearly defined you see it happen in front of your eyes, it happened right there! I couldn't believe it. I had been trying to play the blues since I was 11-years-old and I remember my parents shouting, 'Shut up! What's that noise you're making?' Well anyway the club promoter asked me back the next week."

Spencer realised he couldn't carry on playing on his own and needed a band. "The grapevine network was working well and somebody told me to go and see the Muff Woody Jazz Band. I went to some pub in darkest Erdington and there was Muff playing guitar like Barney Kessell, and little Steve was on piano. He always objected to being called Stevie by the way! But he *was* a Stevie. In fact I always called him Stephen and I think he liked that better. He was 15 and still at school while I was 22. I had already worked in London for three years before I had gone to University, playing at places like The Gyre And Gimble and The Nucleus. When I saw Muff's band I knew I wanted to work with them, but I didn't want their trombone player. I wanted Steve. And Muff came along as a bassman. At that time I saw Steve more as a guitarist rather than a keyboard player.

"But Steve played pretty much everything from guitar to piano and bass. Then we needed a drummer and I immediately thought of Peter York. I had been working with him in the University's Excelsior jazz band, doing an interval spot on 12-string guitar and then singing New Orleans tunes with the band – George Lewis stuff."

The first rehearsal of the new band was held at Muff and Steve's parents' house in Atlantic Road where there was a piano they could use. "It was a damn sight easier going there, and Muff also had an ancient tape recorder. In fact I still have one of the tapes of the rehearsals! I also have a tape of a recording session we did in a pub in Birmingham of the original Spencer Davis Group, when it was still called The Rhythm And Blues Quartet.

"I've got one of the tapes with Muff's handwriting on the back. Muff used to ferry Steve around to rehearsals and gigs and kept an eye on him. I don't think Steve was too thrilled about that, but he was very young to be put into something like a pro band. It's just that the talent was there and he could sound like a genuine blues singer when he was only 15. When he sang 'Georgia' he had Ray Charles' vocal sound and Oscar Peterson's piano phrasing. I thought Steve was astounding."

With the impossible situation of a schoolboy turned musician it was considered best if Steve left school as soon as possible, at the age of 15.

"We had started playing at The Golden Eagle with Spencer and we had done one or two of these all-nighters while I was still at school," says Steve. "We played at The Twisted Wheel, Manchester. My parents would let me go basically because Muff was with me, otherwise they certainly wouldn't have let me go at that age and stay up all night. He was a responsible lad but I guess the headmaster got wind of that. He never showed any encouragement although you would have thought the school system would have tried to encourage someone who showed a talent. Instead the headmaster slung me out! His name was Oswald Beynon – not Oswald Mosley! He was a Welshman but we won't hold that against him.

"I had been playing with Spencer Davis and we had been getting some write-ups in the *Birmingham Mail*. He stood up and said: 'Certain members of this school have been burning the candle at both ends.' And that was it. But he let me go back to do my 'O' levels and I got one, an 'O' level in music. It was an achievement but I never went back to pick up the certificate. That was my credentials for life."

Champions of the English Midlands music scene coined the phrase 'Brum Beat', which sounded conveniently like drum beat, to describe the plethora of local groups. Brum derived from the local name for Birmingham, 'Brummagem', a word which was also used to describe imitation jewellery and cheap metal trinkets made in local factories. Hot among the 'Brum beaters' was a well-built, cheerful jazz fan who idolised drummers Gene Krupa and Buddy Rich called Peter York. He was born in Middlesbrough in the north east of England on August 15, 1942. He began playing drums after discovering a pair of wire brushes at the age of 10 and soon afterwards saw legendary swing giant Gene Krupa in a movie which proved a source of inspiration.

Pete studied drumming in school jazz groups, and later played in an army marching band and student symphony orchestra. Leaving school he worked as an apprentice at engineers GKN but he also played drums with trumpeter Eddie Matthews in Birmingham University's jazz band. "I wasn't at the University but I used to go there and play several nights a week," he says. "The guy who used to sing during the intervals and sometimes with the jazz band was Spencer. He was singing blues with a 12-string guitar round his neck and a harmonica on a piece of bent coat hanger doing what Donovan made a lot of money out of! He was a busking folk blues singer.

"At the same time the Winwoods had their own band which was attached to the arts school in Birmingham – The Muff Woody Jazz Band. Steve played piano and Muff played rhythm guitar. Steve also used to have, on a music stand next to him, a Melodica, which sounded slightly organ-like. He played right hand solos on that and left hand on the piano and then he used to sing. He was probably only 15, his voice had only just broken and was pretty high, but he was singing in a style that was heavily influenced by the people he was listening to, mostly Ray Charles. I sat in with them quite a lot."

If their regular drummer was sick, Muff would call Pete to 'dep' with the band whose front line included trumpet, trombone and tenor sax. "They played some quite swinging arrangements which made it a lot of fun for me to go and play with them," says Pete. "One of the things they did I remember particularly, a Stan Kenton tune called 'Opus In Chartreuse', a lovely piece. None of us was long in the tooth – I was just 20 – but that was the sort of music we liked to hear. Most people wouldn't associate Steve Winwood with Stan Kenton, but we all had our influences. At home my mother had around the house all the old Benny Goodman and Gene Krupa records played on her wind up gramophone. I found a pair of drum brushes that belonged to my cousin. I started banging on pots and pans, as most drummers do!"

Pete, like Steve and Muff, had gone through the skiffle era and played in a Dixieland band. "It was pretty awful I'm sure but we were very enthusiastic and watched everything that came our way in terms of films." Too young to go to jazz clubs, and deprived of jazz on TV the young fans would watch *The Glen Miller Story* at the cinema for the glorious moment when Gene Krupa came on for a drum solo, enduring hours of tedious Hollywood 'romance' for a few minutes excitement. As a teenager Pete was later able to go to all the jazz concerts he liked, and saw Count Basie, Duke Ellington and Woody Herman. One of the biggest impacts was made by veteran drummer Jo Jones playing with brushes and sticks on a JATP (Jazz At The Philharmonic) package show. "I never forgot that. I thought if I'm going to play drum solos, I hope I can make them as interesting as this."

Pete's imaginative, improvised solos later became a big feature of The Spencer Davis Group and with his subsequent duo Hardin And York. He loved his drums and treated them with great respect, insisting that the band's roadie, John Glover, hold the cymbals and drums with dusters, to prevent the scourge of greasy finger prints. Pete also brought his sense of humour to the band which Steve appreciated. With the rest of the audience he laughed at Pete's George Formby routines and comic announcements. It helped take the spotlight away from him, and put audiences in a happy receptive mood. The Spencer Davis Group at its peak developed a whole club show, in which they all had a part to play.

Pete vividly recalls the first time he heard Steve. "There was a pub in Birmingham called The Chapel. On Saturday lunch times, everyone would go down there and sit in for jam sessions the like of which are very rare now. One day Muff came along there and asked if his brother Steve, who was in short trousers, could play the piano. He was still at school and seemed much younger than we did, because four or five years makes a great difference when you are at that age. The difference between 20 and 13 is enormous. So he sat down and played . . . and he was amazing! He had all this maturity and swing to his playing. He seemed to have the whole jazz experience down. One of the reasons was that Steve's father, who is a lovely man, used to play tenor sax. So they always had good music around the house and would listen to Coleman Hawkins and Ben Webster."

Pete was astounded to hear the young pianist playing bits of Count Basie, and even Art Tatum, who was famed for the complexity of his left hand in particular. He could also play in the style of Oscar Peterson. But Steve wasn't a prodigy in the sense of being an astounding technician.

"I remember being very impressed and thinking how remarkable he was," says Pete. "He didn't whizz around the keyboards in a technical way. It wasn't fireworks all the way, it was just a great *feel*. He played all the right things. He later made a classic version of 'Georgia' with us and the piano solo was so mature. It was what you should arrive at, after having done everything else. You knew that Count Basie could play a lot of piano, as he did in the 1940s, like boogie and stride. In his later years he decided to play that wonderful style where he plinked out a few notes that were perfect! You didn't need all the rest. Steve was playing more than the economical Basie style, but he just seemed so mature. In other words, well deserving of playing with us incredibly experienced 20-year-olds."

Pete would thoroughly enjoy the experience of working with Steve for the next few exciting years although he was well aware of the age gap between them.

47

"Steve has got a lot of joy out of life, especially in the last few years. He always had a lot of fun in his life, and always had his mates that he ran around with. He didn't spend too much time with us except when we were on the road, because he *was* much younger than us and it did seem a difference to him.

"He had a great attraction for girls of course, not only because he was the singer, but from the way he looked, especially compared with the rest of us. I think he can thank the rest of us a little bit for that. Ha, ha!"

From sitting in with The Muff Woody band, the turning point came when Spencer Davis was asked to play every Monday night at The Golden Eagle, a pub which has since been demolished. They already had a resident swing band comprising musicians on a free night off from the local Palais de Danse orchestra. They wanted Spencer to sing with them but it didn't work out too well. Spence asked the pub manager if he could bring in his own people. As a result they fired the palais musicians and in came Pete York, Muff and Steve.

"I can't remember if on the very first job Steve had started fooling around with the guitar but Muff played bass, Steve was on piano and Muff's old guitar – from time to time," says Pete. "Muff switched to bass to allow Steve and Spencer to play guitars. For a while Muff did play guitar and they had a stand-up double bass player, but it was finally agreed an electric bass guitar would give them the beefy beat they needed."

Says Muff: "I bought myself a bass guitar and we had The Spencer Davis Group. This was in 1962. We played blues numbers and discarded rock, pop and jazz. We concentrated on discovering rhythm and blues singers so we could plunder their material."

With his Bob Dylan-style harmonica harness, Spencer Davis had quite a reputation on the local scene as a folk singer. Steve was intrigued by Spencer's use of the 'harp'. He explained that he used six different ones for different keys. Steve said: "Oh yeah?" picked up one of the harmonicas and played it. "Here we go again!" was Muff's reaction. Steve also got himself a harness and strongly featured harmonica on many of the band's earliest recordings, playing with the same potency he displayed on all his other instruments.

"Steve quickly became a very fine guitar player," says Pete York. "He's just one of those guys who can pick up an instrument and play something on it. He sat down at the drums and played things for me that were amazing. I even remember him picking up a sax, and blowing it. He could get some notes out, which was more than most could do."

"It was a rhythm and blues club and we played in the upstairs room every Monday night," says Steve of The Golden Eagle. "It was really wild. We had a lot of students there and blues collectors. They were

48

the first Spencer Davis Group gigs. The Chapel pub was more of a jazz club and we had done sessions there with Muff's band on Saturday afternoons. The Golden Eagle was eventually pulled down and in fact the whole of Birmingham was pulled down including The Midlands Institute just a couple of years after I left. It was a beautiful old Victorian building. Someone has some answering to do. Now you get all these 'theme pubs' and of course they've all got black and white pictures of how Birmingham looked before the planners destroyed it. You used to be able to find your way through it – but now you can't."

Spencer had a clear idea of what the new band was going to play even if the rest of them had different influences. "Blues. That's when we had our first policy disagreement because Peter was inclined towards jazz, but all we needed was a real solid off-beat. Pete was into more melodic playing and he did leave the group and we got another drummer in temporarily. I've still got Pete's resignation letter. But it wasn't right without him. Besides that Pete was very funny too."

Before the group began to take off, Spencer and Steve did quite a few folk club gigs as a duo. "We did Sonny Terry and Brownie McGhee stuff," says Steve. "Spence would play a couple of Leadbelly and Big Bill Broonzy songs."

The Monday nights at The Golden Eagle, not far from the Town Hall, became legendary and they also played at the University common room before branching out, playing all around Birmingham. At the same time rhythm and blues had started to become a national craze with the emergence of Alexis Korner's Blues Incorporated, and later The Rolling Stones, The Graham Bond Organisation, John Mayall's Blues Breakers, The Yardbirds and many more groups who would become the backbone of a nation-wide club scene. All the bands were great, and all were different, from Zoot Money's Big Roll Band to The Animals and Georgie Fame And The Blue Flames.

Says Pete: "R&B was really fresh then and I remember a band called Denny Laine And The Diplomats, who later became famous as The Moody Blues. All the members of the Moodies were in various early groups around town. In fact they formed The Moody Blues to play R&B because of the success of Spencer."

"We were playing seven nights a week in Birmingham," says Muff. "We were incredibly popular. We must have been good . . . there were queues down the street. People in Birmingham had never seen anything like it." Television newsmen came along to the pub just to film the queue outside. On another night the band played at Laura Dixon's dancing school, just along the road.

"We had two residencies a few hundred yards apart and then we started getting gigs all round town. We were called just the Rhythm And Blues Quartet which wasn't very inspiring. Later on we decided to

49

use the name Spencer Davis, as he had been the one who put the thing together. Spencer also had a name on the blues scene and had even played in London."

Muff defined this latest example of British kids devising their own version of American music. "It was rock 'n' roll for those who didn't like country blues, and blues for those who had never found anybody who could play it to them before. We had Spencer who was not only a very good singer but had a real knowledge of the subject leading the band, and we also had this kid with an incredible voice, singing some of the songs. Steve very much needed Spencer. He introduced him fully into what black music was all about. They were up-front swapping vocals while me and Pete York used to thump away behind."

The new group led by Spencer Davis found itself supporting the big names in the burgeoning scene including Manfred Mann and Graham Bond's Organisation. The latter group featured Graham playing Hammond organ and alto sax, backed by Jack Bruce on vocals, bass guitar and harmonica, and Ginger Baker on drums. The Bond band were one of the most exciting jazz and blues fusion outfits on the road.

"They were great and had only just started to come out of London," says Muff. "The bands from The Flamingo Club in Wardour Street, like Georgie Fame And The Blue Flames, had just started. They came up to Birmingham University and we were the support. They'd come into the dressing room and tell us we should turn professional as there was a whole scene going on."

The Brummies' heads were filled with wild tales of dates available as far afield as Scotland and dozens of clubs in the London area. Work was available seven nights a week and there was good money to be made.

"In 1963 things were getting quite hectic," recalls Pete. "We were still trying to do our day jobs as well. By the time spring 1964 came along we had already been approached by a couple of people. Decca were interested and we did a couple of demos."

Giorgio Gomelsky, who managed The Yardbirds, had also been making inquiries about the quartet from Birmingham. Giorgio, a wildly enthusiastic and multi-lingual Hungarian emigré, was one of the first promoters to see the potential of R&B and booked The Rolling Stones at the Station Hotel, Richmond, in February 1963. When the band were taken over by Andrew Oldham, Giorgio found another band to replace them – The Yardbirds, featuring Eric Clapton on guitar. Giorgio would subsequently manage The Brian Auger Trinity, The T-Bones and Steampacket which featured Rod Stewart and Long John Baldry. Many years later he would release through the French BYG label several of his private recordings from the mid-sixties under the collective title of The Rock Generation. One of the records featured a Birmingham Town Hall concert billed as 'The First Rhythm And Blues Festival In England' held on February 28, 1964. As well as The Yardbirds backing Sonny Boy Williamson, The Spencer Davis group are on the album playing 'Dimples', their first single. Steve had never heard the recording until he was given a copy by the author of this book in 1989.

It was Spencer who made contact with Giorgio. "I went to The Crawdaddy to see The Yardbirds with Eric. I went up to Giorgio and said I'd got a band that was better than that. I was talking about our band with Steve, Muff and Peter. I told him we played in a place called The Golden Eagle on Monday nights."

Meanwhile Giorgio had set off around the country with the revered visiting American blues man Sonny Boy Williamson. On their way back from a trip to Manchester they stopped off at Birmingham. Sonny Boy staggered out of Giorgio's car with a suitcase full of harmonicas and a bottle of Scotch. Spencer's stock rose overnight when it was revealed he had somehow inveigled the legendary harp player to call by and sit in. "Bob Wooller was the compère and unknown to us Giorgio was busy underneath the stage recording what he later put out as an album! We didn't know about its existence until somebody gave me a copy. Sonny Boy also jammed with us but that wasn't recorded."

Says Steve: "We backed a lot of blues guys later like Memphis Slim, Champion Jack Dupree, John Lee Hooker, and T-Bone Walker. I never really talked or got close to any of them. I guess to them we were just a rather inferior back-up band."

But the potential of the young group was obvious and a crucial decision was made. Spencer's boys turned professional. "We had a struggle to get Muff to go pro. He didn't want to go on the road. Now he flies all around the world," laughs Spencer.

It was the start of years of touring for Steve. "We started to travel all over the country from Newcastle to Liverpool where we played The Cavern. Even in the year before they kicked me out of school I was certain I wanted to be a pro musician. I was actually making money out of it and I wasn't interested in any other kind of job. In those days a band could survive on playing a few gigs a week."

Steve didn't see the band as anything more than just a way to play music. "With hindsight I can see how the group got bigger and bigger but the fact that they were older than me meant there was a different attitude. I didn't want to just keep on reproducing blues. After just a couple of years of that I saw it as a dead-end street. After seeing the greats like T-Bone Walker or Memphis Slim I thought I was never gonna be as great as them. But that wasn't really right either. The Stones and The Beatles started off as rhythm and blues bands and in both cases it very quickly became a different thing. And of course by the end of The

51

Spencer Davis group we were writing our own stuff like 'Gimme Some Lovin'' and 'I'm A Man' and they did actually have our own stamp."

Just as the group decided to make a serious stab at being a professional band they met Chris Blackwell, who would have an important role to play in both the future of the band, and Steve Winwood in particular.

Jamaican born, Harrow educated, Blackwell was in Birmingham for a date by blue beat singer Millie whom he managed and who had just had a big hit with 'My Boy Lollipop'. She was playing in a package show at the Town Hall. After Millie had finished Blackwell asked around: "Is there a decent club to visit? I'm staying the night." He was told about a great local band playing at a nearby club at around 11 pm called The Rhythm And Blues Quartet.

Says Muff: "We still weren't called The Spencer Davis Group at this time. Blackwell came down and saw us and asked to be our manager. It was my idea, well after Blackwell had got us a deal with Philips, to call it The Spencer Davis Group. Everybody was called The Somethings, like The Beatles, or The Animals. Blackwell said we had to use a hard name, like The Rattlesnakes. I said everybody had names like that. Spencer had a good name and he was a great guy for talking to the press . . . so it was my brilliant idea to call it The Spencer Davis Group! It was never Spencer's idea."

"They were terrific times," says Spencer. "I made the move from Sutton Coldfield to Potters Bar and we began playing all the London clubs. We'd play The Shakespeare at Woolwich, The Black Prince, Bexley, Cooks Ferry Inn and The Bromel Club, Bromley. And we'd pack the joints. We were a very entertaining band. We did a lot of one night shows, and yeah we got paid well for those. Muff and I made sure of that. But that was basically our only source of revenue. We didn't know that you got paid for songs on the radio or that there were such things as 'mechanicals' or performance royalties. We had no idea. We didn't have a clue . . . Bands in those days were fleeced left, right and centre. It was abominable. And unfortunately that was happening in the States too."

Spencer, Steve and the band were all too busy having a good time and getting high on the excitement of the times to bother too much with the finer points of business negotiations. "Raving was what it was all about then," says Spencer. "It was the lifestyle. We'd go off on trips to the East End at four in the morning with The Beatles, to have a cup of tea on the Isle Of Dogs! Even the gigs were like a party. You'd have Eric Clapton sitting in and loads of other guys with the four of us, and it would end up like a completely different band.

"During that whole period there was so much going on, so many commitments, there was hardly any time for normal life."

Steve actually seemed to sail through all this first taste of the high life with cool aplomb. It could be viewed as a learning process for Winwood, a kind of rock college with hit records for degrees. But that is a conveniently romantic view of events. Steve sees it rather differently. "No – that's not true. I wasn't learning about the business! I've only just started learning about the business! And I wasn't learning about recording then. I was kinda mildly interested but it wasn't until I was well into Traffic that I started to learn about recording. The only thing I thought about recording was it never sounded as good as it did when you played live. Now of course . . . it's the other way round!"

53

the ravers

The Spencer Davis Group quickly found themselves in a recording studio to make their own version of John Lee Hooker's R&B classic, 'Dimples', which they had now been playing live for some time. "We made a super version of it as our début single," says Muff "but John Lee Hooker's version came out at the same time (August 1964) and became a reasonable chart hit. We didn't get anywhere with ours but we created a bit of a vibe I think."

Pete York: "Unfortunately we picked a moment when promoters were beginning to see the sense of bringing the original blues artists to England."

In 1963 when The Spencer Davis Group were still semi-pro they had already played with Sonny Boy Williamson, Memphis Slim, Jimmy Witherspoon, Champion Jack Dupree, and Charlie and Inez Fox. Pete remembers driving Sonny Boy Williamson back from his flat in Smethwick to his hotel in his battered old Morris Minor convertible. Sonny Boy asked Pete what he wanted to do with his life. "It was one of those conversations you have late at night after you've had a few. I said I wanted to be successful and make some money out of being a musician

. . . I wanted it all! He said to me – 'You don't want to worry. You've got a nice little car, a place to live, a roof over your head. That's all you want in life.' And I thought, 'Oh no it isn't!' He thought I'd got enough already."

The band stuck to their policy of playing blues standards, or tunes dug out from obscure labels and recommended to them by producer and disc jockey Guy Stevens, one of the great record business characters, who put out the Sue catalogue in England. Says Pete: "We played hardly any originals at that point. We did Elmore James' 'Dust My Broom', and all the things that were on our first album were typical of the stuff we were doing live. I've still got the only recording left of a demo we made for our own benefit in a little studio in Birmingham. We had five copies printed, and there were five tracks on it. I've got the only one left. The other guys all had one each and they got broken or lost.

"It's the very first recording of Steve's voice. He was very young at the time but had this amazing feel. We did songs like 'Dimples' which was in the set at the time."

At first the band would play mostly blues but later on, under Pete's influence, they began to attempt modern jazz tunes like Horace Silver's 'Sister Sadie', which they played at The Marquee Club in London. "When we played a residency at The Marquee in 1964 and 1965 we got big crowds and we played all sorts of things, even my George Formby songs! There may have been a few dissenters in the audience thinking why the hell are they wasting five minutes on this? But most people actually went along with it and I've always been of the opinion that you can mix things up in a set if you do it honestly . . . we all thought it was funny anyway." Pete used to sing the gormless Lancashire comic's 'Stick Of Blackpool Rock' and 'Waggling Me Magical Wand'.

"Those were the only ones I did. If I ever did that again, I've got a lot more material now! But all the bands like The Mark Leeman Five and Mike Patto with Time Box used to do gags during the set."

The Spencer Davis Group had a very British sense of humour and all got along well. But there were occasional moments of friction. "I do remember one occasion which was quite a dangerous moment for me," recalls Pete. The scene was the band's famous blue Commer van, fitted out with a limited number of seats. "I had a girlfriend named Lesley. We were going up to Manchester, and anyway we had a kind of politeness among ourselves – we were very considerate to each other – nice, well brought up lads that we were. So if one of us wanted to bring a friend, and take up a seat that might otherwise be used for sleeping, we would ask the other fellows."

Pete remembers asking Muff and Spencer if it was alright to bring Lesley but couldn't find Steve, who had temporarily vanished. "I couldn't ask him, but my girlfriend turned up and duly rode with us in the

56

van to Manchester. But Steve was very upset by the fact that I hadn't asked him and he hadn't been considered."

Pete was worried that Steve might have thought his opinion had been overlooked because the rest of the band were so much older. It was an indication of the hidden tension that the age gap sometimes induced in the otherwise easy going Steve. "We didn't treat him like a kid in the band but I have read interviews since and I think he might have felt this. If he was, then it was unconscious. I always got on with him very well and one of the reasons was I respected what he could do. He was fun to play with. The first thing I wanted him to do when we got to a gig and set up was to start playing something. We had some lovely sessions, before the gig.

"But this was one of those things where I neglected to do something and there was quite a post-mortem over it and I was told by Muff that I really had to be very careful because Steve might get very upset and who knows what might happen, y'know? Muff was quite protective and would be the first to admit it. Bear in mind that Steve was so young he probably shouldn't have been in most of the places we were in. He was underage, so Muff was probably charged by Mum and Dad to take good care of Steve and make sure he didn't fall into the wrong company. I don't know what was supposed to happen to people of 16 in a pub, but Steve was well able to take care of himself."

Steve certainly learnt how to cope with the considerable quantities of booze consumed among hard blowin' blues men – but it took him a bit of practice. One of my colleagues at *Melody Maker* in the early sixties was the very funny and astute journalist Bob Dawbarn who had created *The Raver* column which I later inherited. Bob was a jazz and blues critic with a flair for pungent journalism which he thoroughly enjoyed applying to the pop stars the *MM* was obliged to cover. He was also quick to spot the importance of the rise of British R&B as befitted the man who wrote the sleeve notes for the first British Elvis Presley album.

Unlike most jazz critics Dawbarn appreciated the talents of up and coming players like Eric Clapton and was the first on the *MM* to spot The Spencer Davis Group. Bob held regular parties at his house on Hampstead Heath and was particularly proud of the fact that Steve Winwood had been one of his guests, even when the others included the likes of Dusty Springfield, The Beatles and The Rolling Stones. I came into the office in Fleet Street one Monday morning and called out: "How was the party last night Bob?"

"Oh it was great! Steve Winwood was sick on the carpet." It was the first time I recall hearing about the band, and its star singer. I would later learn that Steve's capacity for 'raving', which earned him regular mentions in *The Raver*, equalled that of Zoot Money, Eric Burdon and many others, including 'The Raver' himself. Most of this was done 'after hours' but Pete York recalls one of the few occasions when partying actually disrupted a gig.

"We went down to Southampton, and Steve and I travelled on the train. It was a very hot day and we drank warm beer all the way down. We had also been in The Ship at lunchtime in Wardour Street. By the time we got to the gig he and I were really quite pissed. We made a complete hash of the evening's performance. The other two weren't too bothered but we were laughing and giggling and making lots of mistakes. We weren't taking it too seriously at all and the following morning there was a strong phone call from the club management to our agency saying we had been bad boys. When you think how bad boys have been *since* then . . .! But there you are, we had a few beers on the train, and we had a laugh and a giggle and probably fell over once or twice, and we were reprimanded . . . severely."

Around the time of Dawbarn's party the band recorded 'Strong Love' a powerful, and ostensibly 'commercial' theme, which gave me an excuse to interview the band for the first time, in the *MM*'s favourite pub, The Red Lion off Fleet Street, now sadly demolished. Despite my glowing reviews, none of their first batch of singles were hits and it looked like The Spencer Davis Group would remain an underground, well respected club attraction. I saw them at The Marquee in Wardour Street in the summer of 1965, and I was impressed.

Intelligent programming was one of the group's assets, and something they could only have learnt from experience. They kicked off with 'Kansas City', sung by Steve who, even at 17, had a very powerful and genuinely authentic blues voice. Spencer took over the vocals for the old standard 'Dust My Broom' and Steve offered a short but lively 'Jump Back' and his own intense 'Stevie's Blues'. 'Working On The Railroad' featured a nice guitar riff from Spencer and a touch of feedback which reminded me of The Who's more explosive moments. The group had a relaxed, non-pushy stage presence, a knowledge of dynamics and a grasp of the all-important concept that sheer noise had nothing to do with excitement, an observation of mine which I made at the time but which would be studiously ignored by bands of all persuasions over the coming decades.

Although live show reviews were of necessity brief in those days of tightly edited tabloid music journalism, more space was allowed for features on a band. The first of a great stream of articles I'd write on what became one of my favourite groups was ironically titled 'The Last Of The R&B Groups?'

I began by reflecting on the time when Manfred Mann were a struggling but sophisticated beat group, when Mick Jagger was an up and coming young blues artist and how fans had shed tears over The Yardbirds and Georgie Fame and his Blue Flames.

Would they all get hits - and when - was the burning question at the time. It was an era when scores of new R&B groups were clamouring for public recognition, and now there were few talented bands who definitely deserved to gain public acclaim and a hit record. The Spencer Davis Group was one of them but despite the enormous regard in which they were held by discerning club goers and fellow musicians, fame and fortune seemed miles away.

Spencer and Steve had met me for a lunchtime drink in a pub off Fleet Street, and it was clear from our conversation that they were part of a happy and dedicated group. They talked lucidly and honestly about themselves and the changing attitudes to beat music by the public and musicians. I asked whether they considered themselves the last of the R&B groups.

"Possibly we are the last," said Steve. "There are still a lot of very good R&B groups but not many are trying to make the chart."

When I inquired as to their ambitions Spencer told me he wanted a hit record so he could buy a house, but Steve said he would spend the proceeds of a hit on a new Hammond organ. He told me that the group's next single would be called 'Strange Love' and that it had originally been recorded by an American group called The Malibus. "We found it through an eccentric record collector friend in Manchester," he explained. "He's on the mailing list of all the obscure record labels."

59

Spencer remarked on the broad range of music that was becoming popular as the sixties came of age, everything from Roland Kirk to jug band music. "The public's consciousness has never been so jolted as it has been in 1965," he said. "Can you imagine if the whole thing folded up... the vacuum it would leave in everybody's social life?"

"Well, I'm still waiting to see Ornette Coleman in a kids' club," quipped Steve as we parted company.

"It took us a long time to get our first hit," said Muff when we talked in 1988. "But the records got people talking about us and we were working seven days a week, sometimes nine gigs a week, because on Fridays and Saturdays you did doubles."

The band slogged on around the clubs and ballrooms, trucking from Manchester to Stoke to play the same night, or to London to play at least two gigs per night, with an early evening show and an all-nighter. In Birmingham they might play a large ballroom in Smethwick, followed by another in the centre of town where they would bump into Denny Laine And The Diplomats now also playing R&B.

Muff: "The M1 motorway had only just been built from London to just south of Coventry and that was it. Everywhere else we travelled by ordinary roads and you couldn't get quickly around the country like you can now. We had our Commer van to get us around, but in any case before we turned pro, from 1963 onwards, there were enough local gigs in Birmingham, Coventry and Walsall to keep us going."

One of the bands they met regularly in Wolverhampton was The In Betweens who turned into seventies glam rockers Slade. Even though national stardom lay some way in the future for these nascent stars, they were all doing very well, and earning much more than they might have with ordinary day jobs.

"We made good money," says Muff. "Oh yeah, you bet! We earned money that no band can do today. This is the crying shame now. We made money and learned our trade at the same time, playing seven nights a week before becoming . . . pop stars! We learned how to deal with audiences, how to play long sets without breaking down. We bought our own equipment and van. I soon earned enough to buy me a Mini van, which then cost £300. But when you think a packet of fags cost two shillings (10p) and petrol was three shillings and sixpence a gallon, then £300 for a van was a lot of money . . . but I could afford to buy it!"

Steve agrees. "Bands could work their way up from the clubs then. I remember in those days the drums were never miked. The amplification was just to bring the guitar up to the level of the drums which were the loudest thing in the room. I saw Roger Waters of Pink Floyd in New York recently and he came up to me and said he had seen me playing at The Manor House in North London, with Spencer, and thought we had a great PA. It was just two 12-inch speakers! Now you see bands play in a small club and all the drums are miked, it's got so complicated. We used to be able to get *all* our stuff in a Mini van, and Spencer's Morris Minor. That's the band, PA and everything. But there was no way people didn't hear. They heard everything. But it's different now and it's a great shame bands can't come up like we did any more. I hope there will be a day in the future when musicians can learn like that, the way we did."

Soon all the band were buying their own cars and the new Commer van cost around £750 (£10,000 at today's prices). They paid all their own expenses and never thought of asking a record company to pay for anything. Today a band has to be subsidised by a label just to play one show. The SDG carried their own equipment, while Muff or Spencer drove to the gigs. It was actually a rather terrifying experience to be driven by Spencer, as the author recalls. One of my first trips on a motorway was when Spencer drove me in the group's van at about 80 mph in fog to Liverpool airport to pick up Steve returning from a trip to Paris. It was a firsthand experience of 'motorway madness', that became a new phenomenon of the sixties, along with the mini skirt and Pop Art.

"We drove all over the country, and I did a lot of the driving until we got mates in to help us. We had a guy called Andy Dunkley who was a great champion of The Spencer Davis Group. He now works at The

Ritz Club in New York. He's probably one of the great rock historians," says Muff. "He used to drive us all over the place."

By now Spencer had moved to London and this caused occasional panics, as Muff recalls: "There were two or three occasions when Spencer drove separately from the rest of us to a gig and either because of traffic or the weather, Spencer hadn't arrived. I'll always remember the first time it happened. We were playing in Grimsby, or somewhere and Spencer broke down. We all came separately and found the place was packed because we had begun to make a name for ourselves. We said to the promoter. We can't play, Spencer hasn't arrived. He said: 'Listen, you guys are in real trouble. You have got to get on.'

"So we sat in the dressing room and worked it out so we would go on as a three-piece. Steve put his harmonica harness on and we did the whole set without Spencer. I sang most of Spencer's songs and Steve sang the rest. We found that Steve was such a good player he could do all the chords and the solos. In those days when amplification wasn't so good, you needed a rhythm guitar to fill out the sound. We still hadn't reached the Cream era when equipment was 200 watts and they could get a bigger sound out of the guitar."

Despite what might have been considered a deadly insult in another band to go on without the star, Spencer took it all in good humour. However the rest of the band felt they could give him a warning. Says Muff: "Spence wasn't upset but we told him that from then on we didn't care if he turned up late, because we could play without him, and *that* upset him! It was around this time we first met Eric Clapton who was 17, a few years older than Steve. Whenever we came to London he would always turn up and sit in with us. That was *some* experience to sit there in that rhythm section. Spencer was on rhythm guitar standing at the back with Pete York and myself. Clapton and Steve used to become the front line and trade guitar licks. Sometimes Steve would play the harmonica, or else he'd play guitar with Eric who was just starting to play his long, wailing blues guitar solos. Used to be fantastic!"

"It seemed as though he learnt to play the guitar totally in about six weeks," says Pete. "One minute he was fooling around and the next he was playing all these wonderful solos. It was a bit of shock for Spence at the time, bearing in mind that Spence was the guitar player and always had been. That was his thing. Suddenly there was this guy playing these marvellous solos! It was a different style though. Spencer was into Big Bill Broonzy and Leadbelly and the old, classic style of blues playing. Now when I play with Spencer these days I try to suggest that he plays 'Trouble In Mind' and things I remember him doing years ago. That's what he really started out with. I've tried to embrace lots of styles as I've gone along but I know the things I play with most heart and soul are the things closest to my beginnings."

61

The author recalls seeing Eric and Steve jamming at The Marquee and felt that Winwood was then quite the equal of Clapton on guitar, with the same kind of blues feeling and fluency. Muff reveals that many more of these jams took place at The Manor House, in North London, then a regular blues and rock club. The Who played there one night when Keith Moon collapsed, drenched in sweat after the gig, and was carried out feet first. He recovered later sufficiently for the author to drive him, John Entwistle and fellow *MM* writer Nick Jones to The Scotch Of St. James Club for further raving until the early hours.

Eric was a founder member of this nightclubbing set. The drinking took place in the hours after the London gigs had finished, usually from around 11.30 pm until breakfast was served at The Scotch around dawn. Steve, too, thoroughly enjoyed the round of mixing with the players who made up this extraordinary fraternity of talent.

He was voted a full member of SLAGS, the Society of Looning Alcoholic Guitarists, a noble company that included Eric Clapton, Jeff Beck and Andy Somers (then with Zoot Money's Big Roll Band and later to achieve fame as Andy Summers with The Police). The SLAGS main activity, between talking about music, was drinking vast quantities of Mateus Rosé, and pounding the tables noisily in the downstairs room at The Cromwellian in South Kensington. It was all great fun, even if it did lead to bags under the eyes and an outbreak of spots that played havoc with press photographs.

When the author spoke to Steve in 1989 he laughed at my recounting tales of the SLAGS. "I don't remember that – at all! Are you sure it wasn't the Society of Looning Acoustic Guitarists? I was a member? Well, whatever you say. So we drank vast quantities of Mateus Rosé? I don't think I want to remember that!"

And there was no doubt Steve also enjoyed life on the road, away from London, where there were more late night clubs to explore in towns like Birmingham, Liverpool and Newcastle.

"Steve loved touring then," says Muff. "But he was a young kid and I think maybe he did too much too young. He was working all that time when he was no more than 16. It was too much for him really. You can't make a teenager a man. You have the same thing in the sporting world. If you push teenagers to a ridiculous degree then it affects their bodies, their muscles and bones don't grow properly. The same thing can happen to your mental outlook. If all these things happen to you during your years of growth, although you can cope with it physically it leaves a scar and he's never been a great one for touring since."

Many got the impression that Steve was in a dreamy state, miles away from the people around him, perhaps even from reality itself, during those years. It might of course have been a simple defensive trick to fend off those who wanted to fuss and cluster round a talented youngster.

"I think Steve *was* in a dream. He was dragged along by the rest of us!" says Muff. "He might never have done what he did if he hadn't had his brother dragging him there. Not that I'm saying he liked that. He probably detested it, and he did towards the end. It affected our relationship. I was turning into the ogre, dragging him out of bed, off to the next gig, 'cos he didn't wanna. And he didn't have any friends. He couldn't go to parties with his mates, or go to the local dance hall and pick up girls. Steve never had any teenage life. He was in a band, on-stage from 15 years of age. He found his girlfriends backstage, not always the best choice. He had no friends of his own age at all and never went to a youth club. He was working all the time, all of those teenage years."

Steve in retrospect doesn't feel that he was quite so badly treated. Asked if he felt The Spencer Davis Group became a grind, with him subjected to a great deal of pressure, he says, "I never found it to be so. I refused to let it become too much pressure."

Steve often surprises with the frankness of his self- criticism. "I wasn't really interested in anything aside from music. And that continued like that right through Traffic until I ended up getting ill in 1972. That was the point where I suddenly discovered there was more to life than just music. I didn't care about the money, I didn't know about the money, as you can probably remember I didn't really care about giving interviews . . . I didn't care whether people thought I was rude, whether I slept in a bed that night, or on the floor. I really didn't bother. I had the kind of Bohemian attitude that most young people go through, and so . . . there was no pressure at all. In fact the pressure came *after* The Spencer Davis Group with Traffic.

"That's when I felt pressure and discovered what it was. I put myself out on a limb with Traffic and I didn't have to think or do anything before. The songs were all there. If there was anything wrong with the repertoire Muff and Spencer would get together with me and say 'Look, we need some more of this kind of song, we've got too many slow songs.' But later with Traffic I didn't have that luxury. I had support in Traffic in lots of different ways that I didn't have in The Spencer Davis Group. But it was easier for me in The Spencer Davis Group because I didn't have much involvement in the decision making. It was all done for me. I was the singer, and business was taken care of for me, whereas it wasn't in Traffic. Because I was younger than everybody they looked after me. In Traffic that wasn't the situation. We were all in it together."

keep on running

In the early battles for success and recognition fought by the enthusiastic young bands on the British R&B circuit, some of their most reliable allies invariably proved to be the road managers. While record companies remained remote executive figures, and producers had little of the power and influence they tend to have today, roadies then seemed in charge of proceedings. They alone were able to shout at theatre managers, fight off fans and crooks, act as minder, nursemaid and psychoanalyst. In their spare time they drove the van, booked train and plane tickets, humped the gear, fixed the stage lights and amps, found the beer and pulled the girls, sewed on buttons, pressed pants and mended guitar leads.

About the only job they didn't do was perform on-stage, and occasionally they did actually win a few fans with their version of the 'roadies cabaret' – going out in front of the curtains, grabbing the mikes and unmelodiously shouting "1-2-1-2".

One of the best roadies during the sixties was John Glover who worked for The Spencer Davis Group, a close and trusted friend of the band, widely liked in the business. Along with Tappy Wright of The

Animals, Baz Marsh-Ward with The Nice, and Gerry Stickells with Jimi Hendrix, he was a 'star roadie'.

In the years following The Spencer Davis Group, John became a fully-fledged manager, and later ran his own record label. Most recently he managed the successful pop group Go West.

Back in 1969 he and Muff Winwood ran the Island Agency while John managed Free, Mott The Hoople and Amazing Blondel. He left Island in 1974 to form his own management company to look after John Martyn, and Paul Kossoff in Backstreet Crawler, which proved a traumatic experience. After Paul died (on an aeroplane flight between Los Angeles and New York in 1976), he took over the affairs of ex-Traffic drummer Jim Capaldi when he launched his solo career. But the tragedy of Kossoff's death and the difficult times that followed, lessened the appeal of personal management and John set up Street Tunes, a record label and music publishing company. He leased the rights to certain masters from Island and Atlantic's back catalogues and released a couple of dozen retrospective albums over a three-year period.

Then he discovered Go West and went back into management, struggling for a year until they were signed by Chrysalis Records. John put up money for demos and recorded a single with the group, 'Call Me'.

Recalls John: "Go West were all Free and Winwood fans. They played at the Prince's Trust show a couple of years ago and at Christmas were invited to Kensington Palace to meet Prince Charles and Princess Di, which was a real buzz. There were 120 people at the party and the first person who walked in the door was Steve Winwood. Pete Cox of Go West had never met him and he was a huge Steve Winwood fan and they spent ages chatting together. Steve turned out to be a Go West fan too! He loved their first album."

The royal couple went around chatting to the various artists, including Steve. Although the rock stars were nervous, Charles put them all at their ease, including Steve who years before would have been completely tongue-tied and would have muttered incomprehensibly to the Prince. But the Steve Winwood of December 1987 was a far cry from the tousle-haired hippie of 1967. John Glover noted the change.

"Cor . . . he was incredibly different! He was much more mature. He was always very shy and it was hard to hold a conversation with him. He'd just say a few words to people he only vaguely knew. Now he's great. With Pete he was in charge of the conversation and he conversed easily with Charles, who by the way was well briefed and knew something about alll the artists. He related how one of Annie Lennox' of Eurythmics ancestors worked at Balmoral as a groundsman!

"Steve was great. He had grown up and matured in the two years since I'd last seen him. He was much more positive, and I told him how much I loved 'Back In The Highlife', which was a really great album.

Above: Steve, aged eight, with father James Winwood on tenor sax and brother Muff on second guitar, with The Ron Atkinson Band in Birmingham in 1956. *(James Winwood collection)*

Above: Steve warming up before a Spencer Davis Group show at The Place, Preston, 1965. *(Johnny Glover collection)*

Above: Island Records boss Chris Blackwell (left) with Spencer Davis in Hamburg, 1966. *(Johnny Glover collection)*

Left: The Spencer Davis Group with Steve (foreground) and Spencer, Muff Winwood and Pete York. *(Pictorial Press)*

Below: Muff Winwood in 1966. *(Johnny Glover collection)*

Above: Spencer Davis (centre) on tour with roadies Alec Leslie (left) and Johnny Glover (right), Hamburg, 1966. *(Johnny Glover collection)*

Below: Steve playing an early Hammond organ with The Spencer Davis group at The Place, Preston. 1965. *(Johnny Glover collection)*

Above: Posing with the mini, the symbol of the swinging 60's. Left to right: Steve, Spencer, Peter York & Muff Winwood. *(Pictorial Press)*

Below: The SDG performing aboard a boat on the River Thames during the filming of *The Ghost Goes Gear. (Johnny Glover collection)*

Right: Steve during Traffic's early years. *(Pictorial Press)*

Left: Traffic in 1967.
Left to right: Dave
Mason, Steve, Chris
Wood and Jim Capaldi.

Below: Chris Wood.
(Steve Winwood collection)

Left: *(LFI)* **Above:** Traffic as a trio. Left to right: Chris Wood, Jim Capaldi and Steve. *(André Csillag)*

Above: *(Island Records)* **Below:** Traffic with Roscoe Gee. *(Island Records)*

We talked about how he was going back into the studio to work on 'Roll With It' and he would never volunteer anything in a conversation before."

John could not quite put his finger on the reason for the change. "Maybe it was his having a new wife, or living in America for a while. Or maybe it was just growing up."

When John first met Steve he was in his twenties and Steve was 16. John was working as an architect at the BBC in the transmitting and theatre department, next door to Bush House in London's Aldwych, the banana shaped office complex in the Strand. One of his responsibilities was alterations and improvements to theatres owned by the BBC. He visited the Paris and Playhouse theatres where radio shows were recorded in front of invited audiences, like *The Joe Loss Pop Show*. Here John got his first chance to see rock groups in action.

One summer he went to a holiday camp and recalls: "I met this character from Birmingham, and we became friends. He was Andy Dunkley, a disc jockey who worked at a club where The Spencer Davis Group played. This was 1964 and The Beatles were seriously happening. All we talked about was music!"

Andy and John formed a group which called itself The Slugs and entered the holiday camp talent contest. "We mimed to old Coasters records played at double speed and we dressed up as The Beatles with Beatle haircuts. Andy was always going on about this band he had seen which he said was the best thing since sliced bread, The Spencer Davis Group who played rhythm and blues. I had no idea what that was at all!"

Several months later The Spencer Davis Group came to London and played at The Flamingo Club in Wardour Street, supporting Ike and Tina Turner. The Flamingo was the home of all the organ-based R&B bands like Georgie Fame And The Blue Flames and Zoot Money's Big Roll Band, mostly managed by proprietors Rik and Johnny Gunnell. The Birmingham lads were booked to back Ike and Tina at the gig which began at midnight and went on until six am. It was John's first taste of an 'All-Niter'.

"I had never been to a club in my life. So I went to see them and thought they were . . . okay! But then Andy dragged me to see them play at Birmingham University, and there was a bird in Birmingham I fancied like mad, so I went. This time I really got to like the group. I had never heard of rhythm and blues at all before. I was into Elvis Presley, and was a pop fan. But from then on whenever they came to London I went to see them . . ."

Glover became friendly with the group and went to see them at The Bromel Club at The Bromley Court Hotel and The Manor House in North London. Then at Easter 1965 after a gig at The Playhouse Theatre near Charing Cross, Muff Winwood told John they were being managed by Chris Blackwell. His brother Steve had left school, and they were now professional. To help them out on tour they would need a road manager. "What's that?" asked John. He would soon find out, in a series of events that would set the pattern for his subsequent career. The group had never had a road manager before and they weren't quite sure what one did either.

"They had a little Commer van they put all the gear in and used to travel to all their gigs. They needed someone to drive the van, load the gear and book the hotels."

John went away and thought about the idea, then informed his mum of his plan to jack in his job as an architect to go chasing around with an R&B group. "She had mild apoplexy. I had been at college for seven years studying architecture, and she had worked really hard to keep me at college because my dad had died when I was 15. I promised her I would only do it for the summer and if it was a complete disaster I would pack up, and return to my job."

John Glover left the BBC – and never went back. When he joined the band as roadie they had released their first single 'Dimples' followed by 'I Can't Stand It'. Although the records weren't huge hits they helped establish the band as serious contenders for a wide open pop scene that welcomed all the wildest music the emerging R&B could throw at it, as long as it had a strong hook, grinding guitars and the band had an image. The Rolling Stones and The Yardbirds had opened everything up so that every group had a chance of becoming chart stars, to be fêted on *Top Of The Pops* and *Ready Steady Go!* And so there emerged a strange alliance of Swinging Londoners, the stars who shared the same canteen and dressing rooms in the afternoon TV recording sessions and went drinking together at the same night-clubs after hours. The Spencer Davis Group from Birmingham with its 16-year-old star singer, guitarist and keyboard player, was quickly assimilated into this exclusive In Crowd. And they proved they could party with the best of 'em. Charging along keeping them on the right track from club to theatre, TV studio to airport, recording session to press appointment, was Johnny Glover, soon to become as familiar to the fans as the rest of the group.

"They were immediately successful inasmuch as they were working seven days a week. We would double at weekends. Play Birmingham Town Hall, and then the midnight set at The Twisted Wheel in Manchester. I spent half my time living in Birmingham at Spencer's house. It was great. I loved it! Then the following year in 1966 we had 'Keep On Running' and 'Somebody Help Me'. It was only then the band decided to move to London. Muff was the last to move!"

The band's method of recording its classic early singles was workmanlike and unpretentious. They recorded 'Dimples' and 'I Can't Stand It' at Pye. The B-side of 'Dimples' was a Spencer composition called 'Sittin' And Thinkin''. In a three-hour session they could record three complete songs. Their début LP for Fontana called 'Their First Album' was released in July 1965 and recorded as a set of single tracks.

It was all recorded on a four-track machine and the 'Second Album', in February 1966, was done in much the same way, in blocks of three-hour sessions. "We didn't spend much time on albums in those days!" recalls John. "There was no budget for them. We were on a four per cent royalty. I remember we did a six-act tour with The Rolling Stones after 'Somebody Help Me'. Unit Four Plus Two closed the first half, Dave Berry was on it, and then we came on just before The Stones. It was the time of 'Satisfaction' and I remember them saying they had a really good deal with Decca and their royalty had gone up to five per cent!"

Steve Winwood took the sudden rush into stardom, sharing a stage with the likes of Mick Jagger and Brian Jones, completely in his stride. It didn't seem to bother him at all, and he had a great way of escaping media pressure.

Explains John: "The fact that it was called The Spencer Davis Group meant that Spencer did all the interviews! Lots of people thought Spencer was the singer. Spencer did sing some of the numbers, but lots of people who weren't familiar with the band would assume that Spencer was the main singer. Steve didn't love doing interviews anyway and didn't like having his picture taken. He was a musician first and foremost and just wanted to play. The great thing about working for Steve was that when people started to hear about him, we'd get piles of musicians coming to see him. Eric Clapton would often come and play with us, particularly at The Marquee, and Brian Auger, Graham Bond, and Jack Bruce would sit in. We often played gigs with The Graham Bond Organisation and Steve would sit in with them."

If Steve kept his cool about pop stardom the rest of the band could not disguise their joy at the changes wrought by hit records.

"It was wonderful," says Pete York. "Suddenly we were going to the airport and flying everywhere, popping off to Paris to do a concert, and going off on tours. The hotels got better and the travelling got better. That was the nice thing and everyone loves to have crowds of people shouting and cheering. That was marvellous."

Apart from jamming with their fellow blues bands, the Spencer Davis crowd would branch out into the realms of big band jazz, sitting in with Birmingham's Johnny Patrick Orchestra. Pete played drums and Steve played piano. They did a concert together at Birmingham Town Hall. They also played at The Hammersmith Odeon on a Sunday Big Band Jamboree.

Says John Glover: "I remember vividly the Birmingham gig and it was a real buzz because it was the first time I'd seen Steve with a big orchestra. He played the whole show with them. It was wonderful. I did the sound and lights, such as they were. I threw a few switches at the back of the hall! It was really exciting.

"Another exciting night was at The Club A Go Go in Newcastle when The John Mayall Band turned up with Eric Clapton. He played with us and they had Aynsley Dunbar on drums and he played with us as well. That was a real buzz. We also did a gig there with Acker Bilk and his band and we played together on a few numbers. That was brilliant. Great fun. We went in the Acker Bilk coach. We had the old Commer and they had this *serious* bus with seats and a bar!

"The big Jazz And Blues Festivals The Marquee organised each year were always good for us too. We used hardly any equipment for them. Spence and Steve had these little amps that I could pick up in each hand. They are completely defunct now. They had one 10-inch speaker in each one! Muff had a Marshall 4 × 12 speaker cabinet which everyone thought was a bit loud. Pete had a Rogers drum kit that wasn't miked and nobody was allowed to touch it without a handkerchief or a cloth!"

When the band played at The Fifth National Jazz And Blues Festival in Richmond in 1965 Steve's 'Georgia' was delivered with such feeling that at least one girl in the audience "was seen crying" according to the *MM*. Steve's reputation among fellow musicians was spreading. He was invited by Argentinian jazz pianist Lalo Schifrin to sing the title song of a film called *The Liquidators*. He broke off in the middle of a tour to meet Lalo (then famed for his work with Dizzy Gillespie) in London, then flew back to Hanley, Stoke-on-Trent, the same day to rejoin The Rolling Stones' tour. "He'd heard me on record and phoned me at the Gaumont in Hanley," recalls Steve.

In November 1965 the band played at The Jazz Jamboree Big Band Bonanza at The Odeon Hammersmith. They were featured with The Johnny Patrick Orchestra, but in the event the group were rather nervous and it was not one of their better gigs. They were at their happiest on the rocking 'Let The Good Times Roll'. However, their interest in working with larger outfits was reflected in an *MM* news story: "Stevie Winwood (17) singer with The Spencer Davis Group hopes to record a solo album with big band backing soon. The Spencer Davis group's new single 'Keep On Running' is released tomorrow (Friday)."

By late November 1965 The Spencer Davis Group were 'in' with the In Crowd, firm favourites on the club, and festival scene, and now they were poised to become chart heroes and national pop celebrities. It was all happening at breakneck speed, and they were enjoying every minute.

'Keep On Running' their fifth single released on Fontana that month suddenly zoomed to number 16 in the *MM* Pop Fifty. The song, written by Jackie Edwards, had a driving beat and clear vocal delivery that was ideal for those hit conscious times when The Beatles had set standards for everyone. In fact, The Spencer Davis Group would actually knock The Beatles off the number one spot a few weeks later.

Only a few weeks before the group had been feeling despondent and convinced nothing would ever happen for them. Their proposed single had in fact been turned down as 'uncommercial' and their LP and EP releases were delayed. Even the offer for Steve to sing the title song in the Lalo Schifrin movie fell through. Muff revealed that Steve had begun to hate 'Strong Love' their previous attempt at a single. "He wouldn't play 'Strong Love' in clubs unless people asked him to. We did three or four versions of 'Keep On Running' including one with Steve on piano. We had no preconceived idea of how to do the tune. The hit version just happened."

On January 8, 1966, the *Melody Maker* carried banner headlines 'Spencer Chases Beatles'. It announced the astounding news that 'Keep On Running' was at number two in the chart, with only The Beatles' 'Day Tripper' blocking them from number one. It was also revealed that an LP 'Second Album' would be released in February, and there were plans for the band to visit America and play at Yale University.

That week Steve talked to me about his development as a multi-instrumentalist. "I came from a musical family, on both my mother's and father's side. But I was never forced into playing by my parents. I first started playing when I was six, picking out tunes on the family piano, and my first job was with my father's band when I was nine. It's a funny thing, my first instrument was piano and then I got hold of a cheap old guitar and started to learn that. When I joined my brother Muff's mainstream jazz band I went back to piano and packed up the guitar. But when I joined the group with Spence I started on guitar again!"

"When the group started we were looking around for a black singer but we couldn't get one. I started singing because we couldn't get anybody else."

Did he consciously strive for a black sound?

"Yes, and the thing was I didn't have to train my voice because I had started listening to black musicians at an early age before my voice broke and started singing during the period when it was breaking, when I was 13. My first musical interests were in skiffle, then trad, then mainstream modern jazz. When the trad thing finished I discovered Ray Charles. Now I listen to everything. I think all musicians should listen to all forms of music.

"I still practise a lot on piano. I'm developing my style on guitar too. I know it sounds like a cliché but I want to be an all-rounder. I have never been a purist and I've never hated pop or anything like that. I just want to play my own music. My old man always told me it's a dicey business, and I know that. but there has never been any opposition to me becoming a musician – only from school. Frankly I can't do anything else!

"The thing I don't want us to do is go like The Yardbirds, playing in ballrooms and I'd hate to end up in pantomime like The Rockin' Berries. I just want to go on playing reasonably good music."

Steve told me he wanted to do an album called 'Stevie Winwood Sings The Soul Hits Of '65', which would feature him on guitar and piano and with brass on some tracks.

I asked Steve if he ever felt surprised at his own achievements.

"Yes I do really. It was a big surprise to me about the voice. I never expected I'd become known as a singer. Lead guitar too. I had always considered piano to be my main instrument, but now I think I enjoy playing them both as much. I've tinkered about with drums as well. When Pete York was having lessons I used to go along with him and sit and listen."

Had the hit changed Spencer, Steve, Muff and Pete?

"I can honestly say we haven't changed. I think we've been a bit spoilt. At every job we get better appreciation. I suppose one day we're going to be disappointed."

A week later the group were number one. 'Keep On Running' was the first number one hit of 1966. Fontana announced sales had already exceeded a quarter of a million. Steve reacted to the news with customary caution.

"I'm rushed off my feet!" he told me. "It's very exciting but I don't think it's so much us knocking The Beatles off the top. They just exhausted their sales. I've written the next single 'When I Come Home', which has got a beat but not so blatant as the last one. It's funny, since the hit, people have suddenly changed in their attitude to us, and now we get the big treatment. They all come running at us, the people that have ignored us in the past. I have a big laugh at it all."

In fact Steve's 'When I Come Home' was delayed until September, and 'Somebody Help Me', another Edwards song, became their follow-up to 'Running'. Recording the single was delayed when Steve became ill and suffered from 'sheer exhaustion'. That was the story given to the press, but says Steve now: "I don't think I ever got ill and suffered from exhaustion in The Spencer Davis Group. Probably if a gig was cancelled for any reason they would put that out as the reason. I wasn't so exhausted I couldn't do shows."

The band set off for a lightning tour of Scotland. At the same time the pressure on the band seemed to unleash a spate of bad luck. Steve's notorious fuzzbox broke down on nearly every major gig including *Ready Steady Go!* and *Easy Beat* and was finally declared a write-off. Their van broke down and when Spencer hired a car to get to Margate for a Saturday gig, the starter motor jammed and he had to wait until two am for an AA patrol. At a gig in Woolwich Steve's vocal mike fell apart in Johnny Glover's hands, and the piano stool collapsed just as Steve was about to play 'Goodbye Stevie'. He disappeared from sight, watched by Lionel Bart and Long John Baldry, who had turned up to see the band at The Shakespeare Hotel. Later the piano itself collapsed and he had to switch to guitar. "There's a jinx on us," claimed Glover.

The band seemed to be churning out hits and all their records were good. It just took the public a little time to catch up, and there was no doubt, after the first taste of success, that the group could oblige with increasingly powerful and commercial cuts that did not compromise their musical ideals. It just meant that their audiences became increasingly a mix of screaming teenagers who wanted to idolise Steve and hard core blues fans who wanted to hear the music.

After 'Keep On Running' was a hit and soon after 'Somebody Help Me' was a number one the band played at Wolverhampton Concert Hall, one of their biggest gigs thus far. They bought a completely new set of Marshall gear, and they had two pairs of 4 × 12 speakers each and a 100-watt amp. With a 200-watt Marshall PA it all seemed incredibly powerful. John Glover found it necessary to put microphones on Pete York's drum kit for the first time, using a bass drum mike and one overhead. There were only six inputs available anyway, and once the vocal mikes had been shared, there wasn't much left for the drummer.

At this time Steve was still mainly featured on guitar, harmonica and vocals, occasionally switching to unreliable club pianos. But then he hired a Hammond electric organ to record 'Gimme Some Lovin'' and was hooked on the roaring power of the instrument that was already the basis of the Bond Organisation, The Blue Flames, Chris Farlowe's Thunderbirds and Steam Packet. Now Steve could get more funk power and could also hide away from the front row screamers tugging at his trousers.

Steve bought an L100 Hammond which lasted right through the rest of his time with The Spencer Davis Group until he left to form Traffic when he acquired a bigger instrument. Certainly the use of a keyboard at the side of the stage kept some of the spotlight off him, and increasingly Steve found pop stardom, at first something that amused him, an irritation. I could understand this when walking with Steve through the front door of a large Midlands cinema. We had just done an interview and he was ready for the night's show. It was typical of Steve that he thought he could walk around anywhere without the bother of security, but this was 1966 and fan hysteria was in the air. As we headed for the glass doors a posse of girls came screaming "Stevie!" and waving autograph books. We were quickly separated as they didn't actually want my signature, and were more intent on removing tufts of fur from Steve's jacket. I felt powerless to hold back the hordes, and regret to say I left

73

Steve to be mobbed as he struggled into the building. He looked decidedly unhappy at the whole experience.

"No, he didn't like it," agrees Johnny. "He always wanted to be accepted as a musician and reacted against that whole tight-trousered pop star thing. He wouldn't walk to the front of the stage and tantalise the crowd, which we tried to encourage him to do, to get the girls going! He was never into that. I would set his mike up close to the front of the stage, and he'd just pull it back! Muff used to tell me to make sure Steve's mike was up-front and he'd just take it back. Pop stardom was the furthest thing from his mind. He just wanted to be a player."

But nevertheless as a 16-year-old who was by now constantly in the weekly music press, from *Disc* to *Melody Maker*, *Record Mirror* and the *New Musical Express*, not to mention the glossy monthlies like *Rave*, he had to smarten up and try and look the part. He was good looking and because of his shyness and reticence, there was something of an air of mystery about him. He was never rude or difficult with reporters, and once he could be persuaded to relax, he often had plenty to say. When it came to politics or the state of the music business or current pop controversies, he would turn to Spencer, who could cope with such matters.

"We did get Steve to wear kipper ties," said Johnny Glover, "and we once bought a set of matching grey and blue jackets, and yellow shirts. I had to look after a wardrobe then! I had to go the dry cleaners because we only had one set of gear and we'd clean it for a special show! When I lived in Muswell Hill, Georgie Fame lived in the next block of flats to me. He used the same laundry. I took in Muff's trousers which were identical to ones Georgie Fame had taken in the same day. I took Georgie's back by mistake and Muff put them on that night for some TV show and realised they weren't his. Later I got a knock on the door and it was Georgie asking for his trousers back!

"We did picture sessions for pop magazines, but we never looked at the pictures afterwards. We would do a session outside *Top Of The Pops* or in Germany, where we did a lot of work."

After 'Keep On Running' they spent some time abroad because they had many hits throughout Europe. During 1966 they were working virtually every single day playing Sweden, Holland and Germany for weeks on end, and the band stopped travelling in the same old van. The gigs that fans back in England still fondly remember were just the tip of an enormous iceberg of exhausting work. Even they couldn't do everything on their own and extra help came in the shape of another roadie, Alec Leslie.

Recalls John: "After two hits we did The Rolling Stones tour and went back to Europe and travelling together was becoming a problem. There wasn't a lot of room! We had gone up-market with some

Marshall gear, so the band had to get a car, a Morris 1800 or something and we had the van."

The band worked with agent John Martin who would book them in Birmingham on a Saturday and Hamburg on Sunday. They would pack up at Birmingham Town Hall, belt down 170 odd miles to Dover, the Channel port, and cross by ferry to the Continent.

"It was exciting stuff in those days. It taught me a lot," recalls John. "We booked our own hotels and ferries. The agent didn't do any of that." If anything did go wrong, the band would never shout or complain to their trusty roadies. "They were fantastic, a great band to work for," says John. "Comparing them to bands now – they were brilliant. As long as Pete York had his equipment moved by hand – using dusters – he was as happy as a sandboy. If things didn't work, Steve would look at you and sigh a bit. Muff really ran the band. He was the businessman. The one time we had a cross word was when we played Solihull Town Hall and it was one of the biggest gigs we'd done."

After the support band had finished John Glover checked The Spencer Davis Group's equipment and out they trooped on-stage. But John had forgotten to check Steve Winwood's vocal mike. Catastrophe. It didn't work. The band opened up with 'Keep On Running', the big hit all the girls screamed at. Nothing came out through the PA. Steve was singing, but not a note could be heard. John Glover suffered agonies.

"It was a really simple thing, but I couldn't find the fault," says John. "We didn't own a second mike in those days. We couldn't afford spare mikes, they were too expensive. It was a broken lead and it took me the whole number to get the lead sorted out and back on again. The set went down great but afterwards in the dressing room, Steve and Muff said to me, 'We really don't want that to happen again. It was really embarrassing for us. That is the most important moment for us, when we walk out on the stage. Never mind about the support band, you must make sure it is right for us.' "Nobody shouted, but I felt dreadful and have never forgotten it to this day.

Another painful episode happened one night after Spencer and his wife Pauline had been out for dinner with John. They jumped into the group's van to go home and hadn't travelled a few yards when the engine died. "I'd told John to check the petrol and of course he hadn't. We'd run out of gas," recalls Spencer. "I was so determined to get home I started pushing the van to a garage down the road. The next night we had a gig in Sheffield and I started to sing a high note and suffered this excruciating agony." Spencer had ruptured himself with his valiant attempt to get home.

"It seriously affected my performance, I'm sure of that," says Spencer ruefully.

when the screaming had to stop

Rock music developed at tremendous speed during the middle sixties. In the wake of The Beatles' and Stones' chart successes, the world was hungry for 'pop groups' of any kind. It didn't matter whether deep down they were sincere blues crusaders or secret jazz 'moles'. As long as they had long hair, the right clothes and guitars they were all 'beat groups' in the eyes of the media and ripe for exposure on TV, radio and in magazines. As long as the bands could boast a few hits they were welcome to share the same airtime and concert platforms as the ballad singers, pop stars and 'scream age idols'.

And so The Spencer Davis Group, normally happiest playing Ray Charles' 'Georgia' or Leadbelly's 'Take This Hammer' were recruited to join the big pop package shows and play their 25 minutes-worth of hits. And their hits were just as good as anyone else's on the scene. Although the band never got to America, and missed the age of Monterey Pop and Woodstock by a hair's breadth, they were, as we have seen, hugely popular, especially on the Continent, that huge land mass just 22 miles across the Channel. Britain still couldn't quite believe it was in any way connected.

The group did one huge tour of Europe with six other bands. The headliners were Dave Dee, Dozy, Beaky, Mick and Tich, together with Unit Four Plus Two and German band The Rattles. They played in 20,000 seater sports halls, the biggest venues they had yet experienced. Steve Winwood found himself projected as a pop star in the music press, alongside the likes of Twinkle, Wayne Fontana, Tom Jones and Herman of Hermits fame.

"Dave Dee was the big draw then," says Glover. "We were big but he was enormous. We did a three-week tour with him, very long for us and we played Hamburg where the promoter was having problems with the kids going wild and jumping up and down on the seats. It was early days and people were still nervous about that kind of thing. He had to pay for any seats that were damaged."

During 'Gimme Some Lovin'' Glover was invited on-stage to play tambourine as he'd played it on the record. He had also clapped on 'Keep On Running' and played the gong on 'Strong Love'. "I used to love to hear those bits on the records but I just played tambourine on one number on-stage behind a live mike. It was the number when they all went potty and I remember the promoter running up and tearing the mike off me. He started making an announcement in German. I freaked out, knocked the guy over and grabbed the mike back! I was furious."

John then went out the front of the hall to see what was going on. He found a kid had jumped from the balcony on to the stage and landed right beside the PA column, an early example of stage diving.

"He fell as he landed, grabbed the PA column and brought the whole lot with him. The entire side had fallen over. The guy hurtled off into the crowd. My blood was up and I dived into the crowd after him, and grabbed him. This circle opened around him and an enormous German kid stood up beside him, who was his mate. He was about 10 foot tall! But then my mate Alec arrived and we whipped this guy back stage."

Muff and Steve were watching all this from the stage and said afterwards: "We thought at any minute you were all gonna die!"

Quite often the power would go off, especially in France, or the equipment would just break down, but the band played on, as an acoustic outfit. As long as there was a piano, Steve could cope, jamming with Pete York on drums. They'd switch to Ray Charles' 'Nobody Loves You When You're Down And Out' and did a version that sent shivers down the collective spines of their fans.

On electric guitar many believed Steve was the equal of Eric Clapton for technique and feeling. "I did too," says John Glover. "Yet he never really rated himself as a guitarist. He had a semi-acoustic Hohner for years. I always thought he was a wonderful guitarist. When he could afford it he had a matched pair of white guitars, a Fender Stratocaster and a Telecaster which he kept for years. He bought them after the hits." John has a different view of the group's earning capacity from Muff: "Things were tough in those days. We didn't have any wages coming in and we didn't get a lot of money. We were going out for £100 a night. Even when The Spencer Davis Group got very big it never earned more than £600. Top whack! I was on £30 a week – serious money. I was extremely pleased with that. Sometimes I got expenses from Muff!"

John Glover's attachment to The Spencer Davis Group meant that his promise to his mother to return to 'proper work' was broken. One day she came home to find Steve Winwood asleep in her lounge.

They had finished a late gig and there was no hotel available. John and Steve just crashed out at Mrs Glover's abode. Pete York and Muff Winwood were scattered around the rest of the house, comatose. She was somewhat alarmed by the spectacle but whenever she sees Steve on TV now she tells everyone how the famous Mr Winwood once slept on her sofa.

"Big deal!" smiles John. "After I had been working for them, for about a year, it was my 21st birthday. She had a party at The Green Man in Muswell Hill for me and invited the band and Rod Stewart came along. She thought they were all very charming and polite, and was especially pleased they had given me the day off for my party because we just didn't have 'days off'! She really liked the band. I remember taking her to The Regal, Walthamstow, when we were touring with The Who. She came – with my Grandmother and Grandfather! Ha, ha! We got them seats in the front circle and they had never experienced anything like it. All the kids did was scream and the little girls were looking at her. They all thought she was Spencer's mother."

The screaming was a hangover from Beatlemania and all bands with chart hits were given the same treatment, a reaction that would linger on throughout the decades, accorded to P. J. Proby, The Walker Bros, The Monkees, The Osmonds, T. Rex, David Cassidy, The Bay City Rollers and into the age of Wham! and Bros. The screeching then was like the wailing of banshees and quite unnerving and frustrating to anyone who actually wanted to hear the music. Many of the pop artists accepted it as their due and would have been worried when it stopped. Steve Winwood hated it. Says John: "He found it very, very annoying. That's why we got a bigger PA – so he could be heard. He was very much a pop star, and don't forget he had a string of hits, one after another."

During the Swinging Sixties, the beloved Beat Boom was epitomised by the TV show that used to go out to the nation every Friday night with the cry, "The weekend starts here!"

Says John Glover: "We used to do *Ready Steady Go!* all the time." This was the pioneering British rock show, screened in black and white, that was home to dozens of bands, from The Who to The Beatles, Stones and Animals with memorable guest spots by visiting American soul and Tamla Motown giants like James Brown, Otis Redding or The Supremes. "Vicki Wickham the producer put us on live. It was a completely different game compared to today."

It is easy to look back on the early days of rock with lager-frosted spectacles, but there's no doubt much fun was had and the participants formed a close knit brotherhood.

John agrees: "The road managers and the bands were a lot closer than they would be today. The band relied totally on us. Things had happened so quickly. And us roadies had to be on the ball, especially when they were playing with six other groups on the same bill each night. Things *had* to be right. At the same time we were close friends."

Nowadays the roadies work from eight am to showtime, setting up mountains of equipment and might just see the band briefly when they go on-stage, then they work until three am packing up. It wasn't like that with The Spencer Davis Group. "We travelled with the band. And I used to hold the record for getting out of The Marquee. We could do it in 15 minutes. Club manager John Gee would announce: 'You are now going to see the fastest roadie alive!' It was great, I used to love us playing there. I'd even get Pete's drums out at high speeds holding them with the dusters."

Sometimes they played as many as *three* gigs in one night. They would start out at Birmingham Town Hall, and end up, via Stoke-on-Trent, at The Twisted Wheel, Manchester. In London they might gig in the centre of town, at The Marquee when it was in Soho's Wardour Street, and then head north across town to Tottenham to play a venue called Club Noreik. Somehow Steve survived the routine, but he would often look tired, distracted and dishevelled. Many were worried about his health, but there was no serious drug scene then. Most musicians enjoyed a drink – and a smoke – and that was it.

"Steve coped with life on the road very well," says Glover. "Remember we are talking about the pre drugs-era. Drugs was very much a taboo subject. The Spencer Davis Group were a very clean living band." They were certainly 'clean', but the combination of constant travelling, broadcasts, recording sessions, interviews and a seemingly endless round of gigs took a heavy toll on their nerves. Surprisingly, the normally urbane and unflappable Spencer himself began to show more signs of worry and nerves than Steve. Shortly after the madness generated by 'Keep On Running' began, Spencer met me for a chat in a German-style beer keller in Soho. He was in a pensive mood as he discussed the group's progress and the advantages and disadvantages of having a hit single.

"Having a hit record was the projection of our utmost desires," Spencer told me. "What we all hope is that just because we have had a number one, the kids don't expect us to keep on doing phenomenal wonders in the chart. If we don't have another number one they'll say we are slipping. I don't want 'Keep on Running' to be our only record. That hit got all out of proportion." He went on to bemoan the pressures that the band had to face now that they were pop stars with a chart hit, and looked back with affection on the days when they were a respected R&B outfit and nothing else.

Spencer described wild scenes at clubs where the audiences had changed from dedicated R&B fans to young girls who screamed at the group. "Girls tear us apart and run all over the place. The clubs don't know what's hit them," he said. "Once Steve's guitar disappeared while we were playing and when he got it back there was a girl hanging on the end. But the screamers pay their money to come and see us and they've got the right to do what they want, within reason. At one place like the inside of a Boeing 707 hangar about 25 girls fainted, and one girl was crushed with two broken ribs. It was frightening and Steve didn't want to go on."

Nevertheless Spencer insisted that the group still felt the same sense of purpose about their music. "We want to fulfil people's expectations. I'd like to apologise to people where our gear has broken down and we haven't been able to give our best. The thing I like least is having to do about 10 things at once."

It was apparent that Spencer was in need of a break from the day-to-day pressures of being in a pop band. "After all this tearing about I just want to crawl into a hole for a while. I want to go to a pub with some mates and forget it all for a few minutes."

There was little chance of that. The madness would start all over again when they released their follow-up single to 'Keep on Running'.

I was in the studio the night they made 'Somebody Help Me', the Jackie Edwards song selected as the follow-up. It happened in February 1966. I met up with the band at a picture session in Oxford Street at the height of the rush hour. Then I drove with Muff and Spencer to Spencer's new house at Potters Bar in a limousine that belonged to The Rolling Stones which was on loan to the group. Steve, meanwhile, had gone in search of The Who's Pete Townshend who had a flat in Soho, at the corner of Wardour and Bruton Streets, where he made demos in his mini-studio.

Spencer's wife Pauline cooked us a meal while we watched Jimmy Smith, the jazz organist, then at the height of his popularity, on TV. Come midnight, it was time to drive back to the West End in Spencer's Triumph Vitesse.

The studio was close to Marble Arch and when we arrived Muff and Spencer went off in search of milk and hamburgers. Steve, who had arrived before us, was playing a slow Shirley Scott blues on an imposing grand piano, and only the timely intervention of an ashen-faced recording engineer prevented Muff and Steve from dumping their food on top of it.

81

The meal consumed, Steve stopped doodling and the band prepared for work. The backing tracks – guitar, bass, drums and keyboards – had already been recorded and all that remained was the vocal. Steve had the words written in red ink on a scrap of paper which he placed on a music stand. He would sing lead while Muff and Spencer joined him on the chorus, and he took charge, explaining the parts and intonation. Soon the three gathered around a live microphone, swaying to the beat and singing their hearts out.

'Somebody Help Me' had a lighter touch than 'Keep On Running' and the lyrics – about a 'little boy of 17' – were written with Steve in mind. Their malfunctioning fuzzbox was replaced by vibes played in unison with the guitar, and a touch of bongos was added to the drum track.

It took only a few takes to complete the session and everyone was well pleased with the result. "Whad'ya mean, a number one?" laughed Steve when I told them they had a chart topper in the can. 'When I Get Home', a new song written by Steve, had been chosen as the B-side, but I thought at the time that it was worthy of being an A-side. (It was eventually released as their seventh single in September that year). This needed some editing – some superfluous bass drum beats had to be wiped – and Muff disagreed with this decision. "You want it, you can have it," the hard pressed engineer told him, dumping a spaghetti-like cluster of tape over his head.

The session over, it was time to go for a drink and we all headed for the Cromwellian club in South Kensington where we were greeted by The Animals, Viv Prince of The Pretty Things and P J Proby. Soon Steve was up on stage jamming on guitar with The VIPs, Brian Auger and Long John Baldry. The number they played, requested by Animals' singer Eric Burdon, was the old Little Richard stand-by 'Lucille'.

Many of Steve's best performances in those days occurred during these impromptu jams which were witnessed principally by other musicians and music biz ravers. No one ever thought to capture such moments on tape.

"Expect this to be a giant smash," I wrote, reviewing the single when it came out in March, backed with 'Stevie's Blues'. One week after its release it leapt into the *MM* chart at number four. "You're joking, I'm absolutely knocked out," said Steve when I called him with the news. 'Vote For Spence' was the headline devised by the *MM* and the following week they were number one. Even their biggest fans were amazed at the speed and strength of their success. These were the days when the scene was dominated by giants like The Beatles, Stones, Kinks and The Who. A number one hit was crucially important, and meant big tours, TV, and nationwide exposure. Getting so high meant a band had almost attained Beatle (i.e. god-like) status.

STEVE WINWOOD

I spent most of my time on the phone each week tracking the guys down to hotel lobbies or airport lounges for quick quotes for the front page, never more gladly devoted to a band. In fact Spencer was ill when they had their second number one. He had been rushed to his dentist for treatment for a gum infection. Later he told me: "Now we're a two hit wonder! I'm lying in bed at the moment and I'm going to bolt all the doors before all hell breaks loose. There are people banging on the front door already. The *MM* was the first to predict it would be a hit. It's come as a genuine surprise to all of us. It makes us feel much surer of ourselves. I hope we can do it again."

That week the group appeared on BBC TV's *Top Of The Pops* but whereas a band in a similar situation today would be headlining a tour of major venues and would cancel all other engagements, The Spencer Davis Group were still playing small venues – like The Carousel Club, Farnborough.

While Steve sometimes appeared distracted, he had a close grip on the music, was very shrewd about people and relationships, and wasn't one to suffer fools gladly. Normally patient, smiling and polite, he could get irritated, cross or frustrated. He had a real musician's 'cool', that mixture of dry humour with a certain wariness which warned people not to patronise him or take advantage. He was also a shrewd judge of character, as he proved when I once asked him to describe the other three members of the group. He surprised me with his frankness and insight.

Steve described Spencer as a 'typical University student' because he was fond of using long words which nobody ever understood. "I first knew Spence in Birmingham as the man with the 12-string guitar because it was such an uncommon instrument in those days. He loves folk and he still does, and he digs all that Appalachian music.

"He's a very good singer although he doesn't seem to think so himself. It's interesting that lots of people say we are beginning to sound alike but I can't tell. My own singing always sounds different to how I imagine it, when I hear the records. It's to do with where our ears are in our heads."

Steve had kind words to say about Spencer's affable nature. "He gets on well with everyone, although he can be businesslike when we need decisions. What usually happens is we are bombing along in the car and arguing about money or work and Muff has a big go, Pete mumbles, then Spencer says, 'Hey, but listen fellas. I think …' and we all agree. But he can be very easily influenced by other people. He hasn't got a lot of self-discipline. Supposing Spence should really be going to Birmingham for something important and somebody says, 'Hey Spence, let's go to a party'… he'll go to the party."

Drummer Pete York was responsible for the group's sense of humour, said Steve. "He's always been the funniest member of the group and we all dig his fantastic George Formby imitations. When he does numbers like 'Waving Me Little Magic Wand', it breaks everybody up at the end of a set. When somebody broke into our van which was filled with thousands of pounds worth of gear, they left everything untouched but stole Pete's Formby lyrics and his scarf. Amazing. If there is ever a row in the group, it's less likely to be with Pete than anybody else. He just gives up half way through."

Steve told me that as far as group decisions went, Pete usually hung around in the background and rarely committed himself. "He's very interested in writing and maybe he's got a future there. He went to grammar school which makes him a bit different from the rest of us, confidence-wise, and he's also very conscientious, especially about playing the drums. But I think he should stick his neck out a bit more. He won't stick long enough with an idea, and it's very easy to change his mind."

Turning to his brother Muff, Steve said he was largely responsible for shaping his tastes in music. "I always got to like what he liked, and it was through him that I started enjoying modern jazz when I was about 13, and good music generally when I was even younger. I don't think Muff exactly encouraged me to take up instruments because I always enjoyed playing so much anyway I didn't need any encouragement."

Although the two brothers had always worked together, Steve said he couldn't see any real similarity in their personalities. "Maybe because we are brothers we can't see our similarities. We get on all right and the reason is we avoid each other. I go out and he stays in. It's the best way because we see so much of each other through work anyway. It can be a bit tough because Muff is an introvert and I don't think I am. Maybe I am introvert sometimes. Muff is very narrow minded and rigid in his opinions and the trouble is he's usually right. Muff is such a businessman and really enjoys doing the books."

I don't recall the impact these pen portraits had on the rest of the group at the time, but they were done with care, and honesty.

Ominously it was around this time that rumours began to circulate that Steve Winwood was preparing to leave the band. Early in 1966, just days after the success of 'Keep On Running' the *MM* ran a front page story headed: 'Spence Hits At Stevie Rumour'.

It was the last thing I wanted to hear about the band but there was no ignoring the story, especially as the *MM*'s news editor was pressing for confirmation.

The story referred to rumours that were affecting the group within days of their finding national success, and the main topic was whether or not Steve wanted to stay with the group or branch out on his own. Spencer refuted the rumours when I spoke to him that same week.

"Well the only rumours that haven't gone around yet are that Muff Winwood is leaving the group," he told me. "Muff is very much in love with his fiancée Zena and it's conceivable that one day he will want to marry and leave. These are all things we would work out among ourselves. This is nothing new – group changes are things that have been done before but there is absolutely nothing to these rumours about us at the moment."

Spencer was realistic about the group's longevity. "Let's face it ... it's obvious that what we are doing now is only going to last for so long. We can't go on being popular for ever and ever – Amen. Steve wants to record an album on his own, when he gets the time and if he goes solo it will be furthering his own career. I don't see why any individual in the group shouldn't feel free to do this. Steve is the main member of the group. He's our image if you like. He's out front and all the kids go for him. He's a nice little boy, except when he's raving it up!"

For the moment the rumours were set aside. Steve seemed happy, the hits were coming and the band seemed on an unstoppable upward climb. Their success opened up all sorts of opportunities which they wouldn't even have dreamed about back in The Golden Eagle days. One of them was a part in a movie for the whole band. As it turned out *The Ghost Goes Gear* was a contender for a whole new category – the C movie – but it was fun to make, and if nothing else provided a filmed record of the band playing 'Georgia' in the age before video.

The Ghost Goes Gear was a pop comedy filmed on location at beauty spots around the country. The author went to watch the action and found the band looking fit from all the fresh air, discipline and exercise involved in early morning calls for outdoor filming. It seemed they spent most of the day balancing on leaky paddle boats, up to their knees in muddy waters. Their co-star was game show host Nicholas Parsons (a cult figure even then), playing the role of their manager. He didn't seem too pleased at the thought of getting his clothes in contact with the contents of a ditch, but Pete York was obviously enjoying every minute, splashing about in front of the cameras, and perhaps fulfilling his dreams of becoming an actor or stand-up comic.

In the scene I saw the band were performing in a boat going down the Thames. Somebody threw Pete's bass drum overboard. It fell on a duck which headed it into a ditch. The boys chased after it in paddle boats, Pete navigating in a bath. The bath sank and so did Pete. Thus far the boys had filmed when I joined them. Later they encountered a ghost. The boys took up action positions in the ditch. Steve, wearing a spotless white and blue check shirt and immaculate blue jeans, was carried to the middle and dumped on a sandbag by a technician wearing filthy shorts and waders. Pete, in the uniform of Admiral Nelson, was squashed into a paddle boat held steady by more technicians – also in filthy shorts and waders. Two men arrived carrying a cage filled with ducks. A brand new bass drum was hurled in the river and kicked to pieces. Six more lay around on the bank waiting to be wrecked.

It all seemed very silly and I could tell by the expression on Steve's face that he agreed. Twenty years later he still hadn't changed his opinions about the band's venture into movie making. "That to me was disastrous, the worst bit of management possible. I don't know what he (Chris Blackwell) was trying to do, getting us into that," he said.

"It was an abysmal movie. I only agreed to do it as long as I didn't have to talk. But I still thought at the time that it was the stupidest thing, and since then it has seemed to me even more stupid. It was a very good example of extremely bad management. It was obviously something The Spencer Davis Group should not have been doing. It was Blackwell's idea. He set the deal up. I know Pete had a talent as an entertainer, and maybe he wanted to do something like that . . . but I don't think so really!"

I eventually saw the movie in an empty Odeon Cinema in Peckham in South London supporting *The Hoodlum Priest*. The best moment came when Steve sang 'Georgia'. The sole reaction amongst the cinema audience was an old lady in the stalls loudly proclaiming "disgusting!"

Years later Muff hired the movie for The Spencer Davis Group reunion dinner, and loud were the guffaws. At least it presented a filmed record of Steve singing one of his favourite old standards at a time when videos were non-existent. "But it was mimed anyway," reveals Steve. "There is German TV stuff of us playing 'live' in that period which has a good sound. The film was really just a mistake."

the split

The summer of 1966 was a hectic time. Cream had formed, Bob Dylan played at The Albert Hall watched by The Beatles in a private box and The Stones released 'Paint It Black'. Every day, it seemed, musical history was being made.

Towards the end of a busy year, The Spencer Davis Group released their third album 'Autumn '66' complete with hideous cover. I was slightly disappointed by the package and thought they could do much better. However it served to introduce Steve's increased use of Hammond organ which he featured on 'On The Greenlight', and there were two great Winwood vocal performances, 'Together 'Til The End Of Time' and a cover of Percy Sledge's 'When A Man Loves A Woman', his best work since 'Every Little Bit Hurts'. My review grumbled: "For some incomprehensible reason the sleeve design is demonstrably dull, possibly in an attempt to prevent too many people actually buying the album."

They should have made a much better album at this crucial time in their career, especially since they were planning their first visit to America. Many such plans were laid but none came to fruition. While the band were more popular than ever, there was an indefinable sense of something wrong. The loud clamour of rumour of a split had been discounted, and nobody was saying anything officially, but simply by talking to Steve you could tell his thoughts were way ahead of The Spencer Davis Group. I met Steve for lunch when 'Autumn '66' was released in September.

In the subsequent article I announced that Steve, now 18, was at the "crossroads of his career," when he had passed the 'boy wonder' stage and was now a musician who had achieved much in a few years. My intro may have sounded like the American Declaration of Independence because, of all the artists and great players who had blossomed in that exciting period, I thought Steve had the greatest innate talent and potential. Whatever the future held, I saw him as a solo concert artist, singing, playing guitar, piano, and organ and backed by a big, powerful band of musicians, technically his equal, who could provide solid, sympathetic backing. We would have to wait 20 years before we saw Steve in the setting I visualised then.

Back in 1966, in a restaurant in Wardour Street, just before The Spencer Davis Group took the stage at The Marquee Club, Steve told me about his immediate future. "I've suddenly realised how much I've got to learn musically," he said. "There's no talk about the group breaking up at all now, but obviously the time will come when it does break up and when it does I'd like to spend six months just learning and studying to become a better musician. The last time I studied anything was four years ago. I can't sight read but I know the structure of music and given time I can write a small arrangement. I want to write arrangements for bands like The Hobbits and Wynder K. Frogg. I've got as far as I can without study and I've been static for at least two years."

Steve wasn't happy about the 'boy wonder' tag which had been bestowed on him, and cited this as a reason why he hadn't improved as a musician. "If someone would come up to me and tell me I'm crap I'd start going places. In fact I have experienced some criticism. Things have been slung around about my guitar playing."

Steve was keen to improve on his keyboards and also wanted to try vibes and drums. He was anxious to be recognised as a musician and not a pop star. "I've experienced both and I'm not too keen on the pop star bit," he told me. "I go along with it - I'd be a fool if I didn't and I feel more confidence because of it all, but I still get embarrassed a lot. I get mobbed but mobbing depends a lot on how you carry on. If you run out to a great big waiting car, then obviously you'll get mobbed. But if you take it casually kids won't bother you. Obviously I like having fans, but when they start doing silly things it brings you down."

Steve appeared concerned about the future of The Spencer Davis Group, and expressed his dissatisfaction with the choice of singles that were being released by their record company. "We're losing our sense of direction. The numbers that we want never get released as singles. But basically we're still all heading in the same direction to be musically good and progressive, rather than just being screamed at. One of the things I dislike is narrow-mindedness in music. I don't like people who say: 'Well, I just play jazz man.' A lot of musicians have gone like that. I want to stay in music of all sorts because I can't really do anything else. My current influences are Roland Kirk, Charles Mingus and The Beatles. I've got very interested in The Beatles' work just recently."

I wondered what Steve's ideal band would be like. "That's very difficult because my mind keeps changing all the time," he said. "It would have to be small with a big band sound. With a big band everything would have to be written. It would be difficult to keep the musicians interested and together, if they were just employees and didn't have much freedom to improvise themselves. But I could do a lot of big band stuff on record. I feel at home in a recording studio."

Steve was in two minds about the current success of 'When I Come Home'. "I feel a combination of happiness, frustration and boredom," he said. "I'm looking for new material all the time, and I'm trying to write but it takes time, which is something we don't seem to get much of."

I told Steve I thought 'When I Come Home' was something of a throwaway number, and it appeared as if the group had lost interest in it from the recording. "Well, it was edited," Steve told me. "It was a lot longer originally and I was quite interested in it. You probably thought that because the song was in a lower register than usual and it's not such a raver as the last two. We recorded it as a B-side a long time ago. We'll be damn lucky if it gets to number one."

Steve often looked bad tempered and moody on stage at this period of his career and I asked him whether this was a reaction to the screaming that went on in the crowd. "Bad tempered? Oh yes! But I've only ever walked off stage once and that was in Norway. It was out in the country and all the locals brewed their own moonshine and got terribly drunk before the concert. We'd all been bitten by mosquitos and weren't feeling up to much anyway. Then a fight started during the concert, the bouncers went mad and Spencer's mike got knocked over, so I said, 'That's it' and we walked off."

In November 1966 Fontana issued 'Gimme Some Lovin'' which was a big hit for the band. John Glover remembers that it marked the first appearance on the scene of one of "Steve's Birmingham mates," drummer Jim Capaldi. "He was involved on the percussion track and on the follow-up 'I'm A Man'. He played the African drum. This was where the Traffic thing started. I still don't know what caused the split funnily enough. Steve just moved on. What I most noticed after that was he became a tremendous user of talent. When he played with somebody who was good, he drew from that person's experiences and expertise and then he'd get bored and move on. He's a huge talent himself, and I've always been a fan. But towards the end of The Spencer Davis Group you saw that he could play with a variety of people. When he did jazz gigs people said, 'Hey, who is this guy?' He could play their style wonderfully well and the old jazzers would agree he was seriously happening.

"Before Traffic was launched he did the 1967 *NME* Poll Winners concert at Wembley," continues Glover. "There were 30 bands on the bill. Steve did a Nina Simone number on his own on grand piano. I picked him up that morning because he was then living in Aston Tirrold in Berkshire, with Traffic. They were forming the band. I went to get him, then picked up Chris Blackwell. I was driving the car and we had a crash on the way up. It was raining and we were passing through Maidenhead at 70 mph, and the car just left the road. We spun three times, went down a 20-foot embankment and just stopped in front of a wall. I remember Chris Blackwell, who was very cool, saying, 'Oh dear, this could be a problem,' as we were spinning round. We all got out unhurt but the car was wrecked. We got a cab to Wembley and Steve went on and played straight away."

John was a "trembling wreck" and later had to go home to recover from shock. He was amazed to see that Steve could just go on-stage in front of 8,000 people completely unperturbed, alone for the first time in his career, and play. "And he was wonderful. Really brilliant . . . I've still no idea what caused the crash and Steve never said a word about it. He just played the gig. He was a very cool person too!"

Although everyone guessed one day Steve would want to branch out on his own, the split when it came was a blow to the fans and of course to the rest of the group, Spencer in particular. A warm hearted, jovial man, he seemed knocked sideways by the fact that suddenly everything they had built up together over the years was taken away. He felt uncertain, insecure and aware that those who were perhaps coldly indifferent to the band and knew nothing about its origins felt he was a figure-head. That was unfair. Spencer had put together the working environment in which a singular talent could develop. There had never been any restrictions on Steve, and Spencer had never tried to hog the limelight. But whatever the facts about the set up, the way it was perceived and subsequent developments created problems for Spencer that took him a while to overcome. Steve, on the other hand, had no such problems, and could only see the logic of his new step, and was thoroughly excited about the challenges it presented.

John Glover: "As I say, I don't really know how the break up occurred. I just remember Chris Blackwell taking me aside and saying Steve was going to leave at the end of that tour."

John was asked to come and work for Island and Muff planned to pack up playing bass guitar and start running the Island agency. John asked Chris Blackwell what Steve's plans were. "Well he's going to put a band together but it'll be ages yet," Blackwell told him.

Glover and Muff Winwood set up the new Island Agency and their first clients were Joe Cocker and Free. The move was obviously a shock for Spencer, as Glover recalls: "Spencer was a bit bitter then towards Chris. We all knew Chris was a fan of Steve's, and that made sense because he was the key talent. With hindsight, if I had been the manager I would have done exactly the same. Steve wrote the songs, he sang and was a stunning musician. It was Spencer's name and he did all the interviews . . . and he was very upset that Chris had gone on to Steve's side when he wanted to leave. So Spencer left Chris Blackwell . . . and carried on The Spencer Davis Group, without Steve. John Martin, our agent, was also a bit upset because he didn't hear what was going on until the last minute either. John Martin managed Spencer, and Peter York stayed with the band for a while. They got in Eddie Hardin on organ and Ray Fenwick on guitar. Alec Leslie, who was by then my brother-in-law stayed with them, while I went to Island.

"The split came as a bombshell to a lot of people, but Steve just said 'I'm not getting much out of this now.' The Spencer Davis Group *had* become restricting to him and he wanted to do more. After years of recording four-track single cuts, his first work with Traffic was to record an album in eight-track, a huge step forward then. Steve was way past songs like 'Keep On Running'. He didn't want to play them any more. He had new mates, Jim Capaldi, Dave Mason and Chris Wood. In the last few months of the old band Steve never went out with Muff and Spence. If we were in Birmingham Steve and Spence wouldn't go out drinking at night. It's quite a small place. If I was out, I might bump into Steve in a jazz club or at the Town Hall blowing with another band, while Spencer would be off to a folk club. You see there was a huge age difference between them and that began to show at that point. Steve wanted to be off with local friends of the same age, and so he wandered into Traffic.

"Apart from the age gap, Spencer's musical ability, not being rude to him, would make a difference. Steve wanted better players around him. It was the same with Muff. He was okay as a bass player but he wasn't the best in the world. Steve wanted more from the musicians around him. The dangers of losing pop success were something Steve wouldn't have looked at. It just didn't occur to him in those days. It might now! He was a musician before anything else, and if he wasn't getting satisfaction from what he was playing, it had to change."

The last Spencer Davis Group hit featuring Steve Winwood was 'I'm A Man' a tremendously dramatic performance with a thunderous beat and massive pumping organ riff that reached number nine in the UK

93

Top Ten in January 1967 and 10 in America in March. Music press headlines hailed their triumph. Then rumours of the split began to escalate. *Melody Maker* finally revealed the full details in an exclusive front page story.

The news broke on March 4, 1967. Specifically, it was now confirmed that Steve would quit The Spencer Davis Group after the current UK tour they were playing with The Hollies ended on April 2.

Manager Chris Blackwell had told me that Steve wouldn't be working at all for some time after he left the group. "He will be very involved in writing and will also be writing songs for films," he said.

Blackwell added that Spencer would continue with the group, enlarging it to a five-piece. "It is impossible to replace Steve with less," he said. "Steve wanted to go away and start his own scene. It's a completely amicable split and both will go in different directions."

It was announced that Spencer would tour America, Scandinavia and Hungary without Steve. Drummer Pete York would stay with Spencer while Steve's brother Muff was expected to "leave and retire from the pop business." After Steve's period for rest and recuperation he would form a new group. The musicians expected to join him in this project would include drummer Jim Capaldi, of Deep Feeling, guitarist Dave Mason and flautist Chris Wood. The name of the new group would be Traffic.

That week I spoke to Steve and Chris Blackwell to get the full story. Blackwell confirmed that Spencer and Steve had been drifting apart, but seemed confident that both could be successful without the other. "Steve will be the one taking the gamble," he said. "Apart from 50,000 hip record buyers in this country the general public haven't a clue who Steve is. It's Spence's name that has been on all the records and they have sold half a million records right round the world. Spencer has the name. It's his face in all the pictures and he has done all the interviews. There is no doubt in my mind that Steve will be successful. He has the talent and Spencer has the talent to spot replacements for Steve. He has already got one or two people in mind.

I was surprised when Chris Blackwell told me that arrangements for Steve's departure had been settled as long as three years ago – when he first signed with the group. "It was agreed Steve would be free to go his own way, when he had solidified the musical direction of his outstanding talent. Steve isn't just a pop star, he has a fantastic voice and musical ability and he looks great too. He's a young kid and with all the praise he has had it would be very easy to stagnate. He's strong enough to realise he could have been a teenage genius who didn't have a chance to develop further. He's not going to become an egghead musician either. When he comes back in October he'll really have something to offer. He's only 18 and he's been working hard for three years and he needs to learn to live like an 18-year-old for a bit, to be his own master and not have to go to a gig and be pulled off stage every night. He's an artist in the true sense of the word."

An enormous strain had been lifted from Steve. He seemed happier than he had for a year when he told me he was writing film music – not a full score but two or three songs.

"There's a deadline I have to reach and it's a bit of a challenge. Actually 'I'm A Man' was originally written for a film for America until we decided to release it as a single."

Steve confirmed that the decision to leave Spencer had been on his mind for a long time. "I've been thinking about this split for two years. I'll be resting for a while at first, although it won't be so much resting as working on writing. I'll just be able to cut out the travelling. I'm not going to study academically but I'll study myself – in my secret retreat."

Steve told me that right from the beginning of his involvement with Spencer it was understood that he would leave one day. "I felt there was nothing more I could do in the group, although as it happens I have left just as we have had a big hit in the States. But I'm prepared to walk out on that. I have no regrets at all and I've learned a lot with the group. I think Spencer will carry on and there's nothing to stop him in fact. I'll be very pleased if they carry on and it hasn't come as a big shock to them. It was just something that had to be done sometime. I felt restricted in playing and I also felt restricted in the way that we were not getting together as a group. Everybody has individual ideas and I think it's better if you put your ideas together. We used to be like that but in this last year we have tended to drift apart. I think a group should live together and eat together and really know how each person thinks."

Steve had clearly been unhappy about his pop star image. "This is my biggest problem," he told me. "How will people accept me after I've left? Like a pop star or as a musician? I'm definitely going to change in a lot of ways. I don't know exactly how but I'm going to change my appearance and my image. It's one of the things that's got to be considered during my time off."

Steve no longer wanted to be an obvious front man with a backing group, as had been the case with Spencer Davis, but this was to be a situation that would plague him throughout his career, a by-product of his prodigious talents. He'd been searching for new musicians for three years, he said, and had some in mind. "It's a gamble and I hope it comes off. I'm going to concentrate on playing the organ and I'll be singing as well. I hope to use everything including vibes. The music won't be like jazz. You won't be able to put a name on what we'll be playing, but 'I'm A Man' is one direction we'll be going in. I'm listening to lots of things in music right now and I've just started getting into Indian music, and John Handy is too much. I flipped when I heard him."

Old favourites would have to go, said Steve, including 'Georgia', a song which had become synonymous with Steve during his years with Spencer Davis. "I tried to put feeling into the song every time when I had to sing it every night but it was getting difficult," he admitted. "I wasn't exactly playing like a machine, but it was more of a mass produced feeling. Really I have enjoyed everything I have done with the group and Spencer but now I don't. That's why I'm leaving."

Although officially it was stated the split was 'amicable' even at the time it was possible to see the effect on the others. Spencer, normally always ready for a chat and a drink, wasn't available when I wanted to ask him his side of the story. Instead I spoke to his gentle and sympathetic wife Pauline who told me: "He's going to carry on. Spencer's a bit worried – that's only natural. He didn't think it was to be so soon."

Later it would become apparent that despite claims the split had been in the pipeline for years, the announcement left the members of the old group dazed and confused. Pete York still recalls the disappointment he felt at the time, and now knows that they lost out on a lot more than the joys of fame.

"The band had gradually worked its way up from a minor hit with 'Dimples' to 'I Can't Stand It', 'Every Little Bit Hurts', and 'Strong Love', on to 'Keep On Running' which actually made it to number one. We had been used to going up. It wasn't overnight success. It took about 18 months which was a nice growing period. When we got to number one it was wonderful. It was a great tragedy the group only lasted another few months after our biggest hits.

"I wish we'd had the longevity of The Rolling Stones and that The Spencer Davis Group had continued, alongside a Steve Winwood solo career. That would have been quite feasible. It seemed so ridiculous, so daft to break up. We'd had a string of big hits and suddenly the group was going to break up. I could not understand why this man Chris Blackwell, who presented himself as our personal manager, didn't get us all into a room and talk some sense into us. He didn't because it was actually to his advantage. He wanted to get Steve on his own. He was the great talent he could make a lot of money out of, and Steve was more easily managed than four of us were. Steve was very happy to be with his mates and go and live in that little cottage where they could think about their music. He had no conception of what was going on. It was tragic really."

Pete was very conscious of the effect that the split up had on Spencer: "We felt so bad about it that one of the mistakes we made was to feel betrayed. Maybe betrayed is too strong a word, but we felt let down.

Why did it have to happen at that point? It was a very gloomy time for us and quite worrying."

Pete thought to himself: "Here we are, we've just made it and we're on the verge of something and now it's all gone! Is there no more music?"

He began to think about going back to find a regular job and Spencer considering becoming a teacher. "We had turned professional, given up all our jobs, had enormous success and then it all stopped."

Many years later, I talked to Spencer about these traumatic events. "A lot of people thought that I was bitter about the premature demise of the band. To a certain extent . . . I was. Because we hadn't realised our full potential, and we had to go back to the drawing board again, including Steve. We'd had a run of hits and then . . . nothing. It was obvious that Steve was going to emerge on his own in one form, shape or another. When I talked to Chris Blackwell about Traffic he said: 'The rest of the guys are over the moon because they've got Steve in the band.' I said, 'They ought to be because the guy is an incredible asset.' I knew he'd move on but it was the way it was done I didn't like. Kind of abrupt. But those abrupt shocks are sometimes what temper you for the rest of your life. It definitely affected me. But I just kept plugging away. Yes I was bitter at the time, but I'm not the kind of person to harbour resentment. I had things to get on with. I had a wife and two kids. I had an offer to come to America in 1970 which I took and have been in the States ever since."

Says Pete: "When the group split up I felt very lonely and out of it. I didn't see Steve and Muff any more, and I couldn't take on big companies. I couldn't afford it. When the break up happened we were separated for a while. And then I was busy getting the new Spencer Davis Group on the road and trying to do something with it, against all the publicity. Most people were saying that now Steve had gone we were finished. We tried to tell them a group with Eddie Hardin and Phil Sawyer could be as interesting, but you take someone like Steve out of a band and inevitably you lose a lot, however good the replacements. It would have been like taking John Lennon out of The Beatles."

In its way, the break up of The Spencer Davis Group was as big a shock to those involved as the later break up of The Beatles. Says Pete: "It was talked about for some time before it happened. I knew Steve liked hanging out with the Traffic guys because they were more fun than we were. I guess we were fairly sedate compared to what was going on with Jim Capaldi, Chris Wood and Dave Mason. At that time pot smoking was a big thing. Spence smoked a bit but Muff and I were brandy and cigars men, who preferred to sit around the club and read P. G. Wodehouse! Ha, ha!"

Although the band came to an abrupt halt and ended Pete's days of pop glory (though not his career as a drummer and bandleader),

97

he can look back on a period of great fun and excitement. "It was terrific and we had so many things happen to us like the chance to make a film. I had a lot of fun with that. We met loads of famous people and remember, because of the hip material we played, we were quite an 'in' group. A lot of other bands would come and hear us play and sit in with us, like Eric Burdon and Alan Price."

The Spencer Davis Group did not immediately die after Steve's departure. "It got on the road again very quickly," recalls Pete, "because the original four of us knew it was going to happen and were all planning ahead. In the final few weeks we were all going through the motions in the sense that we were all waiting and planning for the next stage."

He paints a curious picture of the last days of the band's existence. "On the very last dates we did as the original Spencer Davis Group nearly all the members of Traffic were travelling around with us and hanging out in Steve's dressing room, because by that stage we had separate dressing rooms, and Eddie Hardin was travelling around with us in *our* dressing room discussing our future plans! A very odd situation and not very nice as far as I can remember. I don't think it was very happy."

And so they started the new band with firm intentions. "Everybody said that any success I'd had was totally dependent on Steve," says Spencer, "and I didn't want to spend the rest of my life trying to prove or disprove that." He simply wanted to show that he could be his own man. But one of their first outings with the new band brought home how difficult it would be for Spencer in the years to come.

His new group took on a week of cabaret bookings. They played 'doubles' at The Fiesta, Stockton and The Top Hat in Spennymoor. Groups who had chart success could headline at these up-market supper clubs, a thriving scene where lots of money could be made. The band could book into a hotel for a week, play their set and be much more comfortable than slogging on the road in search of one-nighters. Everything was fine except for their decision not to play any of the songs they'd played with Steve and Muff.

"We thought, this is a fresh new group, so we didn't play any of the hits!" says Pete. "We did mostly new material and of course this wasn't what the people wanted at all. We should have milked all the hits for all we could get, because they were fresh in everyone's mind. But we didn't do it. We wanted a new image. Big mistake. We toured America and of course the only thing they knew about The Spencer Davis Group was that 'I'm A Man' and 'Gimme Some Lovin'' were Top Ten hits! Here we are – The Spencer Davis Group and we don't play 'em. Ha, ha, ha!"

Pete can laugh at the memory because the new band went down quite well, particularly when he and Eddie Hardin played their instrumental version of The Beatles' 'Norwegian Wood' as a duo. Pete, with his grounding in jazz, could play the sort of imaginative drum solo (inspired by Louis Bellson and Buddy Rich) that few if any rock drummers could manage at the time. And this went down a storm, encouraging Eddie and Pete to form their own outfit The World's Smallest Big Band.

In the seventies Peter formed another group with three drummers playing with a brass section. He went on to play with a huge variety of bands and musicians from Chris Barber to the Luxemburg Symphony Orchestra. Spencer began touring once again with Pete York's Blues Reunion in 1985 – sixties veterans who thoroughly enjoyed, as much as the playing, the chance to talk about old times.

Traffic were the first group to 'get it together in the country' when they moved into a cottage at Aston Tirrold in Berkshire, in 1967. It was a practice which eventually became a music business cliché as their example was followed by many other groups who yearned for a peaceful rural environment where they could write music, and escape city hassles and distractions. After years spent inhabiting the twilight zone of night clubs and pubs, 'the country' provided much needed fresh air and peace, reminding tired and jaded young men of childhood holidays, when times were simpler.

Traffic was Steve's brainchild, but his key partner in the project, who came up with the name, was Jim Capaldi, a flamboyant character of Italian parentage, who had a powerful personality, forthright opinions and strong ambitions. Born in Evesham, Worcestershire on August 24, 1944, he started out his career as a singer, switched to drums and also developed as a writer. In later years he launched a solo career as a singer once more, resulting in hit albums and singles.

"I used to sing Elvis songs, Little Richard, Jerry Lee Lewis," says Jim. "Those were the days. You used to hear most of your records at the fairground. I was just music mad." Jim worked in a factory in Worcester for a couple of years but couldn't stand the routine life. He threw his sandwiches in the river one day, and didn't go back to work. Instead he told his mate Dave Mason he was going to be a pro musician.

On leaving school he had a band called The Hellions which included Mason, who would eventually become a key figure in Traffic, on guitar. This band evolved into the pioneering progressive outfit Deep Feeling which featured the innovative use of instruments like the vibraphone, played by Polly Palmer, and the flute played by Chris Wood. Jim played drums and sang at the same time and on arduous trips to Germany would sometimes play and sing for nine hours with only a 10-minute break every hour.

Says Jim: "Deep Feeling was going around 1965. I first met Steve in the second half of '66 when Traffic were getting together. Steve was jamming with us at The Elbow Room in Birmingham that year when 'Gimme Some Lovin'' was number one in America. He used to run around jamming all over the place. I first used to see Steve in a guitar shop in Birmingham. Me and Dave went to see him at a gig one night in a club called Mothers. We were just knocked out, because I had already heard 'Dimples', his record with Spencer, and I thought he was some little old black guy! I couldn't believe he was a 16-year-old kid from Birmingham. We were all sick. We thought – what can *we* do, compared to that? At the time I didn't think we'd get to know him. We were playing acid rock, I guess, having dropped this rather large capsule of strange material from America. In fact it was happening in the Midlands before the West Coast had really got off the ground. I took a tab before playing at The Scotch Of St. James in London with Deep Feeling and went on an amazing acid trip. We started writing songs with titles like 'Pretty Colours', 'The Ruin' and all these weird songs with flute and all that, long before Traffic or Jethro Tull."

Jim is convinced this pioneering Acid Rock was the result of a mysterious visitor to the region, armed with a bag of goodies, who later went on to California to start the scene there. It is a theory which somewhat reverses the accepted version of psychedelic rock history. But then, Jim Capaldi is full of surprising and often mysterious tales.

"Steve was still doing R&B with Spencer while we were doing jazzy experiments. I think that's what hooked him in, as a lot of bands were copying our riffs, and Steve was interested in what we were doing. It was the forerunner of Traffic really. Steve started to sit in and jam with us."

One of the last Deep Feeling gigs was in a French night-club where Jim explained he had to move on. The idea of Traffic developed at The Elbow Room, the club in Aston run by Don Carless which was famed for great DJs and characters.

"They were our kind of crowd," says Jim. "I remember the news coming through one night when Steve was there that 'Gimme Some Lovin'' had just got to number one and we got some champagne out. They were magic days."

Steve remembers The Elbow Room and Don Carless who was usually referred to as Don Carlos. "Carless is a common Worcestershire name but everyone called him Don Carlos because he used to live in Spain sometimes!" Steve went back to play at The Elbow Room in April 1989 to raise money for Don who had been badly burned in a fire. "He needed some help and Jim and I went up there and played with old friends like Trevor Burton who used to be in The Move." The club was by then owned by Albert Chapman, and, says Steve: "By a ridiculous coincidence he was a guy I used to be in the church choir with!"

It must have dawned on Capaldi and his friends that they were luring Steve away from his successful set-up in The Spencer Davis Group, but they didn't really care because they felt they were the future that Steve needed. They were younger and hipper and Steve was excited by the musical challenge they offered. Even so Jim is still conscious of the wounds caused by the break up that the coming of Traffic and his influence precipitated.

"I didn't get any flak from The Spencer Davis Group, but I did from the parents, both Chris Wood's and Steve's. They told Chris Blackwell there was this Italian gangster who was leading their boys astray. I used to cook 'em hash on a little pen knife and get them well stoned. Somehow the rumour got around that I had a knife and I was a gangster. I suppose I looked a bit of a gangster. Chris Blackwell told me later he had heard strange reports about me and didn't know what to expect. He thought I might be some kind of heavy."

In fact Jim is half Italian. His mother, who died in 1988, sang opera and his father played accordion and they used to tour Europe as an act. Jim has a theatre poster of them from their performing days. His sister also sang light opera. Jim seemed to inherit their Latin temperament, and has a strong streak of self-confidence and determination. To some he seemed to dominate Steve, but Winwood too had his own firm views of what should be done and how. He would tolerate situations with apparent amused indifference and then make those radical changes which have so often startled his contemporaries.

"Steve was always so laid-back about things, which is why it is so amazing to see him now," says Jim. "But Traffic was a real band, and not just Steve's backing group. I had the name, which was created on a street corner in Worcester one afternoon. I always came up with the names for bands, and the ideas. I was a sort of catalyst for Traffic. I put it all together and drove it along. I was four years older than Steve. He was 18 and I was nearly 22 so there was quite a difference. We had the same mental outlook but he was very young and I was kinda . . . scoring hash and all that. And I guess I was a little bit advanced in my personality."

Dave Mason, another local musician, who was born on May 10, 1945, was one of the entourage around Steve and Jim. He had already left Jim's previous band several times. "That was a forerunner of what was to come in Traffic," recalls Jim. "He was difficult to work with. He was very much a loner and had strong ideas."

Jim Capaldi had strong ideas too. He wrote the lyrics to their first hit 'Paper Sun' while in Newcastle at a bed and breakfast place owned by a guy called George . . . "where all the bands used to stay" and lived on George's nourishing soup. Jim had seen the title in a newspaper article and wrote the song, partially in his sleep. He woke Steve up and they went into the hotel's front room, sat at an old piano and completed the song that would be released as their début single on Island in May 1967.

"Steve was still on the road with Spencer Davis when we wrote 'Paper Sun'" says Jim. "We were just travelling with him. We hitched into Blackpool when they were playing at the Pier. It was that magical, hanging out on the sand dunes in the evening. Another place we went to was Whitley Court, an old ruin near Birmingham that Bob Dylan came to visit." (The author also visited Whitley Court at five in the morning during that summer with singer Pete Hodges of Birmingham group The Locomotive. It was most certainly an eerie, frightening place.) "Dylan took us all back to a big hotel afterwards, and me, Steve and Dylan sat up talking all night. Steve split at about five am but I stayed until nine in the morning. When daylight came I hitched back to Worcester. The last thing Bob said to me was: 'I hope I haven't been boring you man, but I would have said all that to the wall anyway.' A classic Dylanesque night! No we didn't write any songs. We just sat there, rolling up spliffs."

When the author met Steve for the first time after he quit Spencer it was in a Soho pub and Steve wore a flowing red jacket and the kind of jingling neck bell that had become such a huge craze. He was with the rest of Traffic, whom I was meeting for the first time. They all had that cool, casual self-confidence of the Midlands hippie, which contrasted with the rather more intense, agitated London variety. They talked in a fragmentary fashion, with a sentence starting at one end of the group and finishing at the other.

But Steve, on his own for a moment, was quite incisive. He explained how he was approaching his new role in the band. "I'm trying to lose my old identity and gain a new one. I don't just want to be the guy who sang 'Georgia' and Muddy Waters. I don't want to deny those things, but there is such a lot more I haven't done." Many of his fans thought Steve, who had just celebrated his 19th birthday, had become a recluse since leaving The Spencer Davis Group. He was no longer seen at the old London and Birmingham night clubs, and had hidden himself away at the Berkshire cottage. I guessed that he was actually enjoying his first holiday since the age of 12.

"Traffic just happened really," he told me. "They are all people I knew from The Elbow Room. We played together quite a few times before the split. Traffic is past the blowing stage and we're getting into writing. We've still got problems which is why we don't want to work anywhere until we are ready. When we play after the third single, it's going to sound just as good as the records. When we're ready we're going to play like a complete show. We want to get our ideas over but it will be visual with plenty of dynamics." Traffic wanted to play clubs and concerts but they wanted to break away from the old ballroom network, so long the host to rock bands, but by then regarded as a cultural desert fit only for cabaret appeal pop groups. "We want to prove ourselves to the pop world, but in our own way. We want to make our mistakes in private." (Hence the need for the outdoor concrete stage they had built outside the cottage). "We'll have something for everybody to dig. Our music won't be all like 'Paper Sun'," promised Steve.

Dave Mason told me the song was about a girl who went to Guernsey looking for work and "chased the paper sun."

I asked the band how they spent their time at the cottage. "We sleep!" came the response. "We try to get as much colour into our lives as possible. We see movements and roam through the temple of our minds. We get tripped out with the countryside. It's beautiful." Steve grinned at this and added: "They're starting to accept us in the local village. There is a girl who brings poached eggs out to us from the café and she brings out a couple of horses so we can go riding. But I fell off."

Said Dave Mason: "It's very scary there at nights. You've got to be careful you don't just end up chasing dreams. The life has got its dangers. But as a new way of life, it's as important as the music. We planned the life beforehand, but it can be a volcano. We try to avoid the dangers of boredom and friction. If we get a problem like that we just try to find out what's causing it."

Despite these alleged problems it was obvious Steve was happier than he had been during the last months of The Spencer Davis Group. "That last tour was a big drag for me. The vibrations were terrible. Because I wanted my friends to travel on tour with me they called us 'Steve and his Gypsies'. Gypsies is a nice name, and anyway, *we* don't want to put anybody down."

The Berkshire cottage which became Traffic's base was on an estate owned by William Piggot-Brown who was a part owner of Island Records.

Says Capaldi: "He was a big landowner in Berkshire and owned all of the Fair Mile, the village and some beautiful stud horses. We used to have parties there with Richard Harris and starlets running around the swimming pool. I remember Trevor Burton from The Move coming off the top of a Mini on acid. He broke his arm and woke up in hospital! William owned this huge area of the Downs which included the Keeper's Cottage and he came up with this idea of Traffic having it for five quid a week. Me and Dave Mason used to come down from Worcester, painting it and getting it ready. We all planned to live there, and I must say we were the first group to do that. It gave Traffic a very strong image of us all living together and playing and playing. And that really caught on.

"They had an amazing image of us in America of us all wandering around the countryside. But it was true. Woody (Chris Wood) used to wander around with an Ordnance Survey map looking for ancient burial grounds. And then we'd go home and play some more. There was another cottage just below ours and Joe Cocker took it for a year. People like Ginger Baker would come driving up in Jaguars and get stuck in the muddy tracks. Eric Clapton came down, Pete Townshend, Steven Stills, who was in Buffalo Springfield at the time, Denny Laine. Oh it was an incredible place with incredible things going on down there. We lived there for three years and we kept it going in the seventies.

"We were still hanging out there when we did 'Low Spark Of High Heeled Boys'. Great place, it was just magic. And the music just flowed with us, learning more and more."

Steve would leave the cottage when he bought his Manor house in Gloucestershire where he has lived from 1970 onwards. Another permanent resident at the cottage was John 'Nobby' Clarke, who was not only one of Steve's oldest friends but also his right-hand man who has remained with Steve up to the present day. He is now Steve's manager throughout the world excluding America. He started his career as an unpaid roadie with Deep Feeling and later became Traffic's tour manager after the release of their first album. He first met Steve when both were aged 15. "I used to work with Jim Capaldi and Dave Mason in Deep Feeling," says Clarke. "Gordon Jackson was another friend who is now Steve's gardener and has been for 14 years." Gordon used to be a songwriter and also had a cottage on the Welsh borders where he composed under contract to Giorgio Gomelsky's Marmalade label.

"I wasn't paid for working with Deep Feeling. I was just one of those people who was interested in electronics, and was one of the few who could fix the amplifiers and knew how they worked. Then Deep Feeling split up when Jim went to work with Steve in Traffic."

Nobby was called in to help with the new band. "I saw them around a lot and went to all their shows. Then I moved down to Berkshire and lived in the cottage." Nobby was, in fact, the only true permanent resident as Chris, Jim and Steve all had London flats but they would all converge on the cottage whenever possible.

"We used to do some crazy things. We'd finish a show at around 10.30 pm in England somewhere then drive all the way back to Berkshire, set up the equipment and play again. That's what you do when you're young! That's where all those early songs came from really, just playing and playing and coming up with ideas and lyrics. Songs would evolve rather than come out of people sitting down and writing them. We'd play outside the front door or when the weather wasn't too good, we'd set up inside."

There were three rooms downstairs at the cottage including a kitchen and there were four bedrooms upstairs. A bathroom extension was built on the back. Although it was the hippie era, there were few thoughts of growing their own vegetables. "We used to get out there and cut the grass from time to time but there were definitely no herbaceous borders. There was no need for self sufficiency when the village shop was just down the road."

The band frequented a couple of local inns, one called The Boot which was also used by jockeys and stable lads from William Piggott Brown's racing stables.

In the summer of 1967 I drove down to interview the band at the cottage, accompanied by photographer Barrie Wentzell and producer Jimmy Miller. It was a glorious day. The cottage was small and idyllic, not overstuffed with furniture or people. In fact most of the band weren't there when we arrived except for Steve. There was a small concrete patio in front of the cottage, and set up in the open air was a Hammond organ and Jim Capaldi's drum kit. Steve gravitated towards the keyboards and I sat at the drums. Within minutes we were happily blasting away at a blues jam that seemed to gel really well as far as I was concerned. The roar of the organ and drums echoed across the rolling vista of hills and farms, with nobody to annoy, nobody to complain about the noise and no audience to concern us. I couldn't tell if Steve approved of my drumming or not, but he certainly didn't stop playing. I was in some form of seventh heaven when to my chagrin it was all over. Jim Capaldi strode determinedly up the path towards us. He didn't say "Oi, get off my drums" but he did take over, and show me how it should really be done. Twenty years elapsed before I had another meeting with Jim and the first thing he said was: "Do you remember playing my kit with Steve, down at the cottage?"

John Glover was another regular visitor. "I would make regular monthly trips down and bring in supplies of equipment. I remember delivering a sitar one trip, and echo chambers. They were getting into all kinds of different things. Traffic had started to work on their songs and Jimmy Miller was producing because he had done 'I'm A Man' for Spencer Davis. Guy Stevens was still on the scene too. Then Chris Blackwell put them into the studio to make their first album, 'Mr Fantasy".

Mr Fantasy was allegedly some kind of weird spirit that inhabited the cottage and could be seen materialising in the cover photograph on the album with the band gazing in wonderment at the apparition. John Glover has a somewhat more prosaic explanation. "Mr Fantasy was Albert's dog that lived down there. Albert Eton, a road manager for the VIPs group, looked after them all. He was a lovely character and he had this old white Alsatian, called Mr Fantasy, blind in one eye. He found him somewhere. Just before we did our first Traffic date Albert was badly injured in a head-on car crash in Berkshire. It was horrific. He was only a young guy in his twenties." Jim describes Albert as "the classic roadie of roadies."

In the sequence of Traffic roadies John Glover and Alec Leslie were the first, followed by Albert Eton then Nobby Clarke. "We did quite a few shows together before Albert had his accident," says Nobby. "He had a head-on crash while driving on black ice and suffered severe brain damage. He lived quite a few years afterwards and went back home to Carlisle."

Traffic went to visit him several times but he failed to recognise his old friends and a few years later he died. "He was a real character," says Nobby. "He used to do crazy things. We'd stop at The Blue Boar on the M1 and the place would be full of rowdy football fans and he'd get them all singing."

Sitting in the cottage one night Jim Capaldi drew a puppet guitarist worked by strings. The character had a spiky hat. "I wasn't consciously trying to do anything connected with the song, but I wrote a letter next to the drawing which began 'Dear Mr Fantasy, play us a tune.' It was just a few lines. I crashed out and Steve and Chris picked up on it. I heard this music going down, because some of us would sleep while others were playing . . . I heard this thing while I was half asleep and came down. They played the basic shape to me and it knocked me out. I said: 'Wow, that was that little thing I doodled on a bit of paper.' All the things we did were turned into songs. They were built around where we went and what people said. 'Berkshire Poppies' . . . there were always poppies in the fields. The dog was the white Alsatian that was out of its brain, and *then* we called it Fantasy."

The birth of Traffic coincided with, and became a key part of, the explosion of Flower Power. Overnight the brandy drinking R&B men of yore switched philosophies and stimulants in the movement led at home by The Beatles with 'Sgt Pepper' and abroad by the West Coast hippies who created psychedelia. 'Turn on, tune in and drop out,' was the cry, Traffic didn't want to drop out, but according to most eyewitnesses: "Everybody started smoking dope . . . including Traffic. They were stoned a lot in those days. A lot of that went on."

108

STEVE WINWOOD

Traffic recorded their début album at Olympic Studios in Barnes in West London. At the time a budget of £1,000 for an album was considered reasonable. 'Mr Fantasy' cost around £5,000. Producer Jimmy Miller confessed to Chris Blackwell they had gone over budget in their enthusiasm. Incidentally, they were in Olympic at the same time as The Small Faces were recording 'Itchy Coo Park' and Steve Marriott and his band were guest vocalists on 'Berkshire Poppies'. Traffic recorded the track 'Dear Mr Fantasy' more or less live, using an old stage with all the gear set up. Just after recording the song 'Sgt Pepper', The Beatles astonishing new work, came out. The band bought a copy and were astounded. But they had already done 'Paper Sun' and 'Hole In My Shoe' without having the material released, so they couldn't be accused of being overly influenced by The Beatles' experiments. They were all part of the same 'mind expanding' movement which wrought so much artistic brilliance but later led to many tragedies.

Jim Capaldi remembers the atmosphere at the first Traffic recording sessions. "We got into the studio with Jimmy Miller at Olympic, and we couldn't get any feel in the normal soundproofed booths. So Jimmy suggested we set up at the back 'live' with just a couple of mikes here and there. It was like we were on-stage. We just played a one-take jam and it became one of the strongest things Traffic ever played. It broke new ground, influenced people. It had R&B and yet it was different. I remember hearing it on the radio and I knew it was a classic . . . that whole first album."

For the cover an artist friend from London was dressed up in a hired costume to pose as Mr Fantasy in front of the fireplace in the cottage. "The light was fading so there was a big red wash of colour on the album." The band devised a plot of putting out their first single 'Paper Sun' without saying, in the music paper advertisements, who was in the band. There was only a hint that Steve Winwood was involved. The copy read, "Here is a picture of a number one hit by Traffic." In fact it got to number five in the charts. Afterwards Chris Blackwell took out another ad saying, "Your mistake – it only got to number five." Later, in September 1967 'Hole In My Shoe' reached number two.

Curiously enough, their next big hit, which is remembered as the song that most typified the era, proved a great bone of contention among the group. 'Hole In My Shoe', a Dave Mason composition, was released in August and reached number two in the UK singles charts. As well as being a member of Deep Feeling with Jim, Dave had also been in The Jaguars, The Hellions and Julian Covay And The Machine. He actually quit Traffic shortly after the release of their first album in December 1967, and went to Greece, but rejoined Traffic in May 1968 in time for their next LP. He was a sort of floating member, who simultaneously developed a solo career, and he returned to the fold again to record 'Welcome To The Canteen', before eventually moving to America where he ultimately enjoyed considerable success leading his own bands.

Traffic should perhaps have been grateful to Mason for coming up with a hit, but Jim Capaldi recalls the conflicting passions the song aroused.

"'Hole In My Shoe' was the song that nearly broke us up because it was Dave singing and the three of us hated it! It was so silly and poppy and commercial . . . with that little girl reciting poetry . . . it had nothing to do with Traffic at all. Bits of it did . . . the organ for example. But the record company wanted it as a single. Me, Chris and Steve stuck together as a nucleus and the song caused a big rift within the band. We never played it live, ever. Dave left but then he wrote 'Feeling Alright' and got more in touch with things.

"He wrote some great songs and his writing was brilliant. But after 'Canteen' he was off again. It wouldn't work with Steve and Dave. Dave had found his feet and was much more forward than Steve you see. Steve was a bit . . . I dunno . . . he felt uncomfortable."

It has been suggested that Steve didn't get on with Dave Mason because he was a rival songwriter, that Steve 'couldn't handle' this competition. Says Steve: "Um, the guy who said that got it completely wrong. It was about the way Dave wrote. He would come up and say 'Right, here's my song. Now you do this and you do that. And this is the way it's gonna be, because it's my song.' Well the rest of us, we never worked that way. We collaborated on our writing. Some of the early stuff we did – with Jim, Chris and myself – was all written together. We'd throw things around. I'd never say: 'This is *my* song.' But it became Dave writing songs his way, and the rest of us writing songs another way. It was inevitable that Dave wouldn't agree with the way we wrote songs.

"That's why he left. He went before we toured America. He went to America and then he saw us there and he wanted to have another go, and we wanted to let him. But it turned out exactly the same again. He still wrote songs his way . . . which was fine. Nothing wrong with that. It was just in Traffic we worked a different way."

Steve today concurs with Jim's feelings about 'Hole In My Shoe'. "It didn't really represent us at all, although in England it's what Traffic were known for. Not so in America! The Americans have never heard of 'Hole In My Shoe'. We were interested in blending R&B, jazz and blues, classical music and folk and putting all these elements together and 'Hole In My Shoe' didn't do that at all. It was some trite little song that didn't mean anything. But there's no doubt about it. It was commercial. We just didn't want any of it.

"But the record company felt otherwise. Pressure was on us to do something commercial because since the break up of Spencer Davis,

Traffic hadn't been a very commercial band. The result was that in England the band is always thought of for 'Hole In My Shoe'."

Traffic made their live début playing at The Finsbury Park Astoria (later The Rainbow Theatre) in North London with Vanilla Fudge. They used an elaborate new PA system which was supposed to circulate the sound around the audience. Steve Winwood played a huge Hammond C3 organ which had been split into three, so the keyboards and bass pedals had separate outputs. This enabled him to play the bass lines with his feet.

The show proved to be rather chaotic. Vanilla Fudge came off the tour after the second night following backstage rows, the curtain having been dropped during their set at The Astoria!

Steve has absolutely no memory of any backstage rows. He doesn't even remember them being on the bill. "But I was a big fan of theirs!" he claims. Fudge were deafening and were followed by The Flower Pot Men, who hit with 'Let's Go To San Francisco' and threw flowers at the audience. Among their ranks was organist Jon Lord, shortly to become a founder of Deep Purple. They were followed by Tomorrow, led by singer Keith West, and featuring Steve Howe on guitar, then an underground hero and destined for stardom with Yes.

Finally the headliners Traffic came on-stage. The teenage girl fans from Spencer Davis Group days were strongly in evidence, screaming "We want Steve!" while Dave Mason was attempting to play deep and meaningful music on his sitar.

On one of their early UK tours, the three Traffic musicians travelled around – and lived in – a Land Rover. "We decided that we wanted . . . to live in the Land Rover!" says Steve. The vehicle was the original four-wheel drive, go anywhere means of transport pioneered by British manufacturers and now widely copied around the world. The Land Rover remains a unique and popular vehicle, but in no way could it be described as a comfortable mobile home, certainly not the original somewhat draughty and noisy post-war model. However, after the departure of Dave Mason from Traffic, the remaining crew drove one to many of their gigs.

"We decided we would travel around in it and play at places like Leeds University. We wouldn't stay in hotels. We'd sleep in this Land Rover. We'd try and park in wild places – like Ilkley Moor. Chris was a talented map reader and he would find some place and guide us to it. I remember the night on Ilkley Moor in Yorkshire, very clearly. We played in Newcastle and then drove to play in Leeds. We parked about 10 miles outside the city. There was a stove inside the Land Rover and, as you can imagine, it was very, very crowded!"

It was also cold, yet Jim Capaldi had no trouble falling asleep right away, as was his manner after a tiring gig. Chris and Steve who shared the driving, would stay up all night, Chris plotting more routes on his maps.

As well as finding routes, Chris was keen on tracing 'alignments', those imaginary straight lines which seem to crisscross the English countryside and link up dozens of churches and historical sites. Steve still has some of Chris' maps, including a 1962 Ordnance Survey map of Gloucester, bereft of motorways but covered in ruled red ink lines.

"We'd be up all night looking at maps and listening to music while Jim was asleep." Steve and Chris would stay up until four am before finally dozing off themselves in sleeping bags on the Land Rover's floor. Come the dawn, at first light, they would start cooking eggs on the stove and making tea. Then there would be a tap on the window and a farmer saying 'You can't park here.' They'd have to pack everything up, drive on and try and find somewhere else.

On this trip they arrived at Leeds University car park at seven am but the constant arrival of cars meant they couldn't sleep. "The roadies all stayed in hotels," laughs Steve. "It was a ridiculous situation where the roadies were getting room service and we were stuck in this Land Rover. This was really typical of a lot of things that used to go on."

When Traffic played in Redruth, Cornwall, after the show Chris and Steve set off on walks across the countryside by night, investigating ancient stone circles. Then at day break they would go and sleep on the beach, not getting up until three in the afternoon. "We'd eat a salad, then drive on to the next gig."

Most people would find such erratic hours rather debilitating but Steve has never had a problem about sleeping odd hours. "It's easy to get into late nights, especially when you tour. It doesn't mean to say you get any less sleep. It takes a while to unwind anyway, and it's not unusual to get into a cycle of doing a show that finishes at 11 pm followed by a meal. By then it's three, and then you sleep until midday, get up and go to the next gig."

John Glover was now coping with the tons of new equipment – back in his old role of roadie. "Traffic were very much a group and Steve's role was different from how it was with Spencer," says John. "They were a tight unit and wrote things together. But it was the beginning of the smoking age and I was never into that, and in the sixties if you didn't smoke you were considered awfully straight. You were a bit of an outcast and friendly as I was with Steve, I began to feel an outsider. I became the Man From The Office. I was the 'straight' while they were seriously going for it. All they were worried about was playing. They lived together and played together and didn't worry about being commercial or anything like that. They would play all day long. I'd go down there and hear them play for *hours*. They'd set up and play over the Downs."

Steve seemed more reclusive in Traffic than he had been with Spencer's band, and as a performer he tended to hide behind his keyboard without making any stage announcements. Just the voice would come soaring, unaffected and, if anything, more poignant with the new material, over the PA. But the days of Stevie Winwood, R&B and sometime pop star, clutching his guitar and rocking out to 'I'm A Man' were abruptly over.

"It was the fashion," explains John, "to go on-stage and not look at the audience, and not do any interviews. They wouldn't talk to anybody – except you. The only other person they would see was Linda Eastman – doing a photo session. They just got bombed out and played gigs that lasted two-and-a-half hours! On an American tour we did, they played for hours."

Their first US gig was at the Fillmore West, in San Francisco. They played two weekends running. Traffic travelled in a station wagon that contained the whole band, and a trailer with the equipment. They did a whole US tour in this somewhat bizarre fashion and went down a storm wherever they played. The American fans had heard about Steve as both 'Gimme Some Lovin'' and 'I'm A Man' had been Stateside hits. They flocked to hear Traffic play club gigs alongside Moby Grape, Blood,

115

Sweat And Tears, Grateful Dead, and Janis Joplin's Big Brother and The Holding Company.

"They welcomed us with open arms in America," recalls Jim Capaldi. "It was amazing going to visit San Francisco where we saw The Doors and Jefferson Airplane. The hippies and freaks loved us. Great days and great music. Now it's all entertainment and tarting up and packaging with soap opera stars making records. The eighties are all so different from that era."

"The live shows were very exciting," recalls Nobby Clarke. "You were never quite sure what would happen. They weren't the sort of band to play safe. There was a certain number of songs they did live but there was never a running order and the set would never be the same two nights in a row. The length of each song might vary from day to day. Some of them might get pretty long, so they'd just play less tunes. Compared to today's shows it was *so* primitive. Lights were just so you could see them."

Although much was made of Traffic being a team effort, Nobby is positive that Steve was the leader when it came to the music. "He was definitely the leader, although at the time he didn't particularly want to be. He was the leader and that was the way he was viewed by the public, so he didn't have much choice in the matter. But the most vocal person in the band was always Jim. And he's still like that today. None of them had any say in where they would tour. All they bothered about was what they were going to play and what would be released. It was accepted they wanted to play, so they would go virtually anywhere, and Chris Blackwell was in control."

Although Capaldi was a powerful spokesman, like most drummers he proved a rather erratic driver. Everybody in Traffic was wary of getting in a car with him. When the band went on another US tour, the promoters provided two station wagons. As Traffic came out of the hotel in the morning, Jim would say, "Oh, I think I'm gonna drive today." Immediately the entire entourage would pile into the other car.

After the first US tour Steve brought back to England a new Hammond C3 organ to replace his trusty L100, the instrument that had been at the heart of the sound of so many British R&B bands. The organ achieved its great popularity through the records of players like Jimmy Smith, Brother Jack McDuff, James Brown and Billy Preston. But the instrument itself was too underpowered for use in increasingly loud rock bands. The Hammond C3 promised extra power but it also meant more work for the roadies.

"When Steve came back with the C3 it weighed 450lbs. It had split keyboards and a different amplifier for each keyboard. It was really heavy to move. I always remember Kirk Levington Country Club . . . we had to go up an outside staircase which was treacherous when wet. There were two of us to get the organ up the steps and whoever else we could con into helping us. Steve never actually had to carry it himself. The band never carried anything. They just turned up and played."

Nobby used to mix the band's PA sound and for a long time did it from the side of the stage which was common practice before they started setting up their base camp for lighting and sound technicians in the middle of the auditorium. "I really can't remember the first time I mixed the sound out front," says Nobby. "But when I mixed out front for the first few times and Steve might break a guitar string, somebody would come rushing out to the mixing board with his guitar for me to change the string. It was because I'd always done it."

Nobby's work expanded to the point where he became not only a sound technician but the tour manager, booking the hotels, getting the band from one show to the next and picking up the money from the gigs along the way.

Traffic toured America over 10 times during their heyday and Nobby Clarke and the crew drove thousands of miles by truck. In fact, crew was rather a grand description. On two Traffic US tours there was only Nobby and fellow roadie Viv Phillips to handle the gear, and they were accompanied by Chris Blackwell who kept an eye on things.

Although Traffic never played the two celebrated American festivals at Monterey or Woodstock they did appear at the equally large but less well known Atlanta Pop Festival. Most of the time they played smaller venues. "When we played in New York," says Nobby, "we'd do two shows a night for a week at the Academy of Music and then we'd go out of town to play one big show for 18,000 people. They preferred smaller places but when 'The Low Spark Of High Heeled Boys' was a big hit we ended up playing arenas to 10,000 a night. When we went back to playing smaller places again there was a problem with too many showing up and trying to get into the halls."

Although Traffic became hugely popular, they were never a wildly exciting visual act like their contemporaries The Who or, later, Led Zeppelin. "The only movement was when they swopped instruments on-stage!" says Nobby. "Steve played a fair bit of guitar and at one point, when they played as a trio, he used to play guitar while sitting at the organ, and playing the bass pedals with his feet at the same time. The crowds used to sit and listen and then they went berserk, and then they'd all sit and listen again."

When he played guitar Steve used a Gibson Firebird at first, then changed to a Fender Stratocaster after the Firebird was stolen while they were playing in New York. A truck containing the instruments was parked outside the concert hall and nearly all Steve's guitars were stolen along with virtually everything else.

117

It was during an early American trip that Steve and Chris Wood sat in on Jimi Hendrix's recording sessions for the 'Electric Ladyland' album, released in October 1968. "We were playing in New York and then after the gigs we went to the studio with Jimi," recalls John Glover. "That was a buzz. Hendrix was a bit good too. Traffic and Hendrix had played at the same shows together before."

Eventually the pressure of tending his charges and the constant travel became too much for Johnny Glover. "After the first American tour, on the last day I resigned. It had been a particularly hectic three days. Dear old Chris Wood drove me completely demented. I had been there eight weeks on my own in the States and he was giving me grief. He couldn't find his saxophone bug or something. Oh dear! We had been to New York and Cleveland and back to New York and I had to drive 750 miles – in each direction. I'd had no sleep for three days. I'd just got back to New York in time to set the gear up while the audience were coming in. And Chris Wood couldn't find his saxophone bug, which *he* had to keep with him. His bloody bug! I was so tired, I said that's it, I'm off. It's finished. Over. I've finally reached the end of the old tether here! I went back to London to work for the agency and I didn't go on the road again with Traffic."

Despite the tensions and the hard work occasioned by all the travelling, the States proved a happy hunting ground for the band. Says Steve: "What happened in America in '69 and '70 when we first went was the birth of FM Radio. They basically just played albums and for a band like Traffic who didn't have hit singles, we were the perfect band to fit into this radio format. They provided radio that was like having an album on at home, something that still hasn't been achieved in England. FM Radio gave us a big audience in America and our long tracks like 'Dear Mr Fantasy' slotted perfectly into their format."

The band had a big impact in Europe too and Jim Capaldi recalls a particularly atmospheric occasion in Hungary in 1969. "We did a great gig in Budapest that I'll never forget. Wow, it was brilliant. It was one of the first times we'd been behind the Iron Curtain and they wouldn't allow the fans into the hotel to be near us, or talk to us. When they came to see us play at the Stadium there was this great release of energy. You could still see bullet holes in the buildings from the uprising. And there was a great roar from the crowd, and a flash of electricity from the people. It was like an arc . . . we all saw it clearly."

Steve is particularly proud of Traffic's success in America. "When Dave left and we went to America as a trio, that was the time when we actually were the most successful. It was so flexible and we could play so many different things. We'd think of a song and do it that night, without rehearsal. We'd write things and do them straight away. That endeared us to American audiences. In many ways Traffic is a lot more important than The Spencer Davis Group to Americans. And they didn't know 'Paper Sun' and 'Hole In My Shoe'. They knew us from our album cuts which got played on FM radio.

"The reaction was amazing. We'd never known anything like it! Suddenly we were playing at the Fillmore West with all these great bands and they were all attracted to us like moths around a flame. We were just doing something very different. The Byrds and Jefferson Airplane all had three or four guitars and we'd step up with organ and drums. It was a great time for us around 1967-68. When we went to New York Chris and I played with Jimi Hendrix on the 'Electric Ladyland' sessions. We played on 'Voodoo Child'. I met a guy in Nashville who gave me a tape of all the out-takes of 'Voodoo Child'. Most of the people you hear in the background on the record were sitting outside the studio. We had one run-through of the number and Jimi was just talking us through it. Then we cut it."

After Traffic had established themselves as a trio, Dave Mason, the errant songwriting guitarist, wanted to rejoin the band. Says Steve: "Dave Mason had left over the row over 'Hole In My Shoe' and wanted to write songs a certain way, and not collaborate on joint songs like 'Dear Mr Fantasy' which was written by Wood-Capaldi-and-Winwood. That's the way I felt the group should be writing. Dave very soon decided he didn't want to do that. So he left, we went to the States, and then Dave obviously saw the reception we were getting and wanted to come back. He did rejoin for a few songs, and played the guitar solo on 'Heaven Is In Your Mind'. Then he left again!

"We did so well as a trio in America. We really did take off. But the real high point of Traffic came later with 'The Low Spark Of High Heeled Boys' which came after Blind Faith. It was the biggest selling Traffic album."

In addition to the nucleus of Traffic there were many later recruits, like Rebop the conga player and Ric Grech who played bass. The first version of Traffic actually broke up in January 1969 and there followed the short-lived Mason, Capaldi, Wood And (Wynder K.) Frog band while Steve became involved with Blind Faith. The second version of Traffic was born in February 1970 and included Steve, Capaldi, Wood and Ric Grech. Then in May 1971 American session player Jim Gordon came in on drums, while Jim sang, Rebop (who died several years later) was added on percussion and Dave Mason returned to the line-up for a second time. This third version of the band lasted until December. Traffic Mark IV ran from January 1972 until September 1973 with the Muscle Shoals rhythm team of Roger Hawkins on drums and Dave Hood on bass backing Winwood, Wood and Capaldi. Towards the end of the group's life it became a floating situation with the basic trio occasionally

119

performing on their own or sometimes being augmented by any combination of guests.

"The line-up changes just seemed to happen," says Nobby. "There was never any great turmoil. It was like when Jim stopped playing drums. It just sort of happened. He virtually decided himself. We got Jim Gordon in on drums and Capaldi concentrated on singing. Steve accepted this. That was the strange thing . . . they viewed everything as an experiment. That's why they were never afraid to change the line-up. Steve, Jim and Chris were in it together. It was their thing, and they were prepared to try anything. They would never consider, 'Will this do harm to our popularity?' That wasn't why they were doing it, which is one of the main reasons why, on a business level, they had absolutely no idea what was going on. They weren't interested."

Money slipped through their fingers as a result of this *laissez-faire* attitude as Nobby Clarke confirms. "Instead of capitalising on what they had going in America by only playing huge places, they kept playing smaller venues. They earned some money. They had to in order to keep the whole thing going. You can't sustain a band without a fairly good income but that was never the prime object of the exercise."

Says Jim: "I remember when Rebop joined. We were touring Scandinavia. He came in the dressing room and started playing congas. He was a larger than life character. He started jamming with us and he was brilliant. We said . . . 'Come on stage . . .' He came to the next gig and never left! He was in the band. How many bands could you do that with now? How free and open could you get? That was what made Traffic a great band."

Steve recalls that the addition of another drummer and bass player into the band was an attempt to get a show that was "less volatile" and more stable. Says Steve frankly: "What used to happen as a trio later was that it was either brilliant – or absolute rubbish! Bloody awful." Steve laughs about it now but he explains: "It was hard to face the inconsistencies. So that's why we got in Jim Gordon and Ric Grech. But of course this happened after Blind Faith."

Steve pulled out of one of Traffic's American tours when he became unwell. This was after 'The Low Spark Of High Heeled Boys' had gone gold. "That was really the end," says Nobby Clarke. "But they tried to keep something going. They should probably have either taken a long break or finished there. It was true that the last series of shows weren't that great. It was a shame, really, because I thought they still had a lot to offer."

Steve and Jim are very proud of Traffic which made some great music but at the time many fans yearned to see Steve project more, to stand up and rock out. They would have to wait a few more years, until the New Era of Steve Winwood. In the meantime, there were more tours with Traffic, and interludes with Eric Clapton in Blind Faith, and with Ginger Baker's Airforce. His voice was as powerful as ever, and his playing matured. But Winwood, through perhaps both choice and circumstances, wasn't quite as much in the spotlight as he'd been throughout the sixties.

"Right after Blind Faith we did 'John Barleycorn Must Die' which was one of our best Traffic albums," says Steve. "That was one of the first times I recorded tracks where I played all the instruments."

The famous cottage where Traffic had got it all together was eventually abandoned. "It was one of the estate cottages and I believe the owner wanted to sell the estate and of course he wanted vacant possession of his cottage. We ended up moving out, and in any case the four of us weren't living together, it was a different situation. We weren't kicked out. We just agreed to leave!"

121

when the eagle flies

When Eric Clapton, Ginger Baker and Jack Bruce teamed up as Cream in 1966, they were hailed as a supergroup at a time when the phrase had some meaning. They were the best, most innovative players around, and their arrival on the scene was an inspiration to fans and countless young players. Their influence would help shape rock for years to come.

Eric and Steve Winwood had long wanted to work together on a permanent basis, but Steve couldn't join Cream when he was committed to The Spencer Davis Group. I remember going to hear Cream play at one of their first rehearsals in a church hall in Putney. They played me a slow drag blues, Ginger setting up a marching roll on his antique snare drum while Eric unleashed his 'singing' blues style. It sounded so full of promise and potential, I just wish I'd taped the rehearsal. Alas, it was before the age of cassette recorders and even my ink stained note books of the period have long vanished. What I most remember about the afternoon though was their manager Robert Stigwood looking rather doubtful about the decidedly ethnic material they were playing and asking if I thought it sounded "any good".

The historic session was halted by an irascible caretaker as a bunch of Brownies wanted to take over the hall for dancing around toadstools under the watchful eye of Brown Owl. Just to complete the surreal atmosphere, the whole enterprise, which would result in Cream becoming rock legends, was nearly wiped out before it began. Jack Bruce, driving a van which contained Eric, Ginger and myself in the front seat, no doubt under the heady influence of the hand-rolled cigarette we were sharing, shot out of the yard into the street and was nearly totalled in a narrowly-averted collision with a passing car.

I shall always remember the look Ginger gave Jack and the nervous smile that Eric gave me. I felt quite relieved that I could return to the safety of the *MM* office, while poor Eric would be spending the next year or so enjoying such thrills and spills on the road. The next time I saw him was at a party at Robert Stigwood's house near Regents Park to celebrate Cream's début. He was sitting on the floor, holding his head in his hands. Even then he was displaying signs of doubt about the future of Cream.

Cream played their farewell show at London's Royal Albert Hall in November 1968, then not long after, Traffic split for the first time, after Dave Mason quit, in January 1969, leaving an apparent farewell with 'Last Exit', an album recorded both live and in the studio.

With Cream gone after two years of phenomenal success, the way was clear for Clapton and Winwood to work together. "Eric and I had always talked about playing and the time seemed right," recalls Steve.

They started jamming together and speculation was rife. It was rumoured that the pair would record an album with drummer Al Jackson and bassist Duck Dunn, the rhythm section of Booker T. And The MGs who, together with guitarist Steve Cropper, had formed the backing band for so many famous sixties soul recordings by the likes of Otis Redding and Wilson Pickett on the Memphis-based Stax label.

The set-up was all rather vague, but one thing was clear. Eric didn't want another pressurised commercial situation similar to Cream. But that's just what he would get. The project was dubbed, with heavy irony, Blind Faith, without Jack Bruce, and without Ginger – or at least that was Eric's intention. But the latter was desperate to be part of the new outfit. He begged to join and Eric didn't have the heart to say no!

No one questioned his drive, but Eric was by then looking for a different way of playing and he wanted to get away from Cream-style relentless fury. And so there was compromise from the start which was officially in April 1969. Nevertheless Blind Faith made a superb album, released the following September, which featured Steve singing the moving 'I Can't Find My Way Home'. I went to visit Eric at his Surrey home just before the launch of Blind Faith and, in an upstairs room, found a drum kit set up. It was in fact the room used for rehearsing the new band.

Steve wasn't around, but Eric invited me to have a play, and sitting at the kit, I jammed with him for about half an hour, while he played, as I recall a bunch of Buddy Holly hits which he'd been listening to almost continuously for the previous week or so. A group of hippies sat quietly at our feet, and when I realised they were digging the music and not scorning our efforts, my rapture was complete.

Blind Faith, with Ric Grech from Family on bass, made their eagerly awaited début at a free concert in London's Hyde Park on June 7, 1969. We sat on the grass at the front in the warm sunshine, as sweet smelling smoke drifted across the contented hordes of fans. They say there were 100,000 there, but few were in a state to start counting. It was a wonderful day, and expectations were high. The Third Ear Band and Edgar Broughton, regulars at free concerts, did their stuff, but we only really wanted to see the stars. When the band finally came on-stage, they played well enough, but nobody seemed ready to work themselves up into a lather.

"It was our first gig and to do the first in front of 100,000 people was not the best situation to be in," says Steve. "Nerves were showing and it was very daunting. We couldn't relax like you can on tour."

The afternoon's set comprised 'Well Alright', 'Sea Of Joy', 'I'd Rather See You Sleeping On The Ground', 'Under My Thumb', 'Can't Find My Way Home', 'Do What You Like', 'In The Presence Of The Lord', 'Means To An End' and 'Had To Cry Today'. The music was melodic, mellifluous, but afterwards there was a sense of anticlimax. Everyone thought the next gig would be better, but British fans never had a chance to see them again. They were off to America for a tour that Eric didn't enjoy.

Both Eric and Steve had felt pressurised in previous groups or felt they had to make musical compromises. Blind Faith was meant to be perhaps more like The Band, laid back, devoted to music making and honest statements. Instead, under the aegis of manager Robert Stigwood, they were ensured heavy press exposure and much hullabaloo. To be fair, in this respect he was doing his job. Bands mostly complain when they don't get any publicity. But for whatever reasons, the Blind Faith concept didn't live up to its ideals. The musicians wanted to change direction and style but their audiences were hungry for a kind of Super Cream.

Steve later explained that although they had created an identity for Blind Faith on the album, once on the road they gave in to pressure and gave the fans what they wanted. "And they loved it!" Neither Steve nor Eric had the will-power to pull Blind Faith in their direction, and Ginger was doing his best to keep the band in a Cream groove.

125

After Hyde Park, which was filmed but never released, the band set off for a Scandinavian tour in June. The US tour opened in Newport, Rhode Island, on July 11. They were supported by Free and Delaney And Bonnie, and, as well as their new material, they played Cream favourites like 'Sunshine Of Your Love' to placate audiences who had grown violent and demanding. Eric spent more and more time away from the concept that had become a burden, jamming with the American support group.

During the tour a row broke out about the album cover which depicted a nude 11-year-old girl handling a silver model airplane and some shops refused to stock the record. This was a minor problem compared to the trouble at the Los Angeles Forum show when sections of the audience feuded with police.

By then Eric was openly telling reporters: "I don't think the group is going to stay together very long. Steve is going to do something on his own and I will too."

"I've no doubt they could have been a truly great band," opines Nobby Clarke. "But the pressure was far too great. There wasn't anybody strong enough to say, 'Wait a minute, this is what we want to do.' Somehow they got sucked into touring America far too soon. They only had one album of songs and when they got out there the crowd immediately started to yell for Cream stuff. It became like Cream again, with Ginger playing all these huge solos. Yet the Blind Faith stuff was really fantastic. While Steve went on tour with Blind Faith, I stayed in Berkshire looking after the cottage."

Blind Faith broke up after the tour and Clapton went off to team up with Delaney And Bonnie. This pair turned up at Eric's house in November, where they rehearsed for their début European tour with E. C. Meanwhile, rather surprisingly, Steve joined Ginger in his mammoth project Airforce. He wouldn't appear on-stage with Eric again until he played at Clapton's 'comeback' concert at The Rainbow Theatre in January 1973, with Pete Townshend, Ron Wood and Jim Capaldi.

Airforce was put together by Baker in January 1970 and featured Steve, Graham Bond, Denny Laine, Chris Wood, Ric Grech, Remi Kabaka and Phil Seamen (drums). It was Ginger's 'dream band' in which he paid high wages to the musicians he most admired. The running costs incurred during this short-lived experiment would cause him much financial grief in years to come.

Rehearsals were held at The Revolution Club in London, not far from the Stigwood Organisation's office, where Graham Bond confidently told me that "nobody knew what they were doing." Despite this, when they remembered their cues and codas, the high flying ones produced some exciting music.

The band released two albums for Polydor and also played memorable concerts. I saw them at the first gig at Birmingham Town Hall and berated a loud heckler who shouted "rubbish" by demanding that he try and do better. While Ginger remained as voluble as ever, Steve had grown suddenly quiet and didn't seem as disposed to chat. He seemed strained, even worried. Even when Ginger tried to cheer him up by conferring on him the rank of Squadron Leader Winwood, he could only smile weakly.

"It was interesting trying to get all those people in one place at one time," says Nobby Clarke who worked for Airforce while Steve was a member. "In the band was Phil Seaman, the jazz drummer who taught Ginger how to play – and he used to remind him of it constantly! All the time I've known Ginger, Phil was the only person who had any control over him whatsoever."

During this period his erstwhile partner Jim Capaldi was . . . "Hiding out in Birmingham. I didn't know what to do with myself then . . ." Whatever the rift between them, it wasn't to last long. Ginger's hugely expensive project ran out of steam and money, and the leader went off to find new inspiration and outlets in Africa. Steve returned to his old Birmingham mates and re-inaugurated Traffic.

Steve had begun work on a solo album called 'Mad Shadows' which actually became Traffic's reunion LP 'John Barleycorn Must Die' after Steve invited both Jim and Chris Wood to help with the sessions at the Berkshire Cottage. It was released in April 1970 and was a critical and commercial success, and shortly afterwards the three-piece Traffic toured Europe with Free and Bronco, led by singer Jess Roden, as part of an Island package. Audiences in the Netherlands warmed to Traffic, especially when they realised that Steve was not only singing and playing virtually all the melodies himself but also contributing the bass line with his organ foot pedals.

Ric Grech, a refugee from both Blind Faith and Airforce, was later invited to join the reformed Traffic. Then in May 1971 American drummer Jim Gordon who had been in Derek And The Dominoes joined along with Rebop and . . . Dave Mason, yet again. This version played six gigs and recorded the live album 'Welcome To The Canteen'. The same year saw the 'The Low Spark Of High Heeled Boys' which, says Steve . . . "Became our biggest selling album, bigger than anything I did with The Spencer Davis Group. It was an important album for us."

Steve's illness during the period when Traffic were working with the Muscle Shoals players turned out to be peritonitis, brought on by appendicitis which had been undiagnosed. Toxins built up in his peritoneum between the diaphragm and abdomen. Steve shocked friends when he revealed he thought he had been close to death.

127

"Steve hadn't been feeling too well for a while, says Nobby Clarke. "American doctors told him various things, like he had an ulcer, and then nobody back home could find a trace of it. Then one day he was at home at the Manor House and woke up in pain. An ambulance was called and he was taken to Cheltenham hospital. He had a burst appendix. He was operated on straight away and it was a very close call.

"After this Steve started walking in the country. He'd always done it before but it became serious then, and even now he walks a minimum of three miles a day, taking the dogs with him around the farm. The illness changed his whole attitude towards keeping himself fit."

He was just 25-years-old, and it was time to adopt a new lifestyle. He began to take seriously such things as diet, exercise and healthy living. He told *Rolling Stone* in 1988: "I just stopped living for tomorrow. From then on, through the seventies, I came to terms with the real world. Travelling with a rock band has a certain unreality. You don't know where you are, what day of the week it is. People book your plane flights, pack your bag, do your laundry. If you do that from when you're 15, it's unreal."

When Steve recovered, the remnants of Traffic adjourned to Jamaica to record 'Shoot Out At The Fantasy Factory' and undertake another world tour. But some reviews were less than enthusiastic, in particular a harsh *Melody Maker* review of a Traffic show at New York's Academy of Music which did not please Chris Blackwell. Chris Wood had begun to drink too much and his playing suffered. I last saw Steve with Traffic at one of Britain's annual rock festivals, and was sorry to see a lackadaisical performance of material that was somehow gloomy and joyless. Much of the fun had gone out of rock music for a whole generation of confused young players.

The show, at the annual Reading Festival on the banks of the Thames on August 31, 1974, turned out to be Traffic's farewell performance, although nobody, except perhaps Steve, knew it at the time. There was no great public pronouncement or headline news. Traffic just came off the road and never went back.

Steve told *NME*'s Angus MacKinnon in 1977: "I suppose I just split the group. We were half way through an American tour when I couldn't handle it any more. I've never felt there was much point in doing something unless you can really put your heart into it. Maybe I am a little impulsive about these things, maybe I don't always give proper notice of my intentions." Steve denied he was being irresponsible. He had good reasons. "After we reformed Traffic I made it clear I was going to be the group's leader. And groups have to have leaders, otherwise they lose sight of their objectives. The final decision was mine. We couldn't have gone on for much longer anyway. There were various personal problems which are best forgotten; there wasn't the cohesion to keep it together. Traffic had been going for such a long time I wasn't committed any more."

The live album 'On The Road' had appeared in October 1973 followed by their last album 'When The Eagle Flies', recorded at Steve's home on an eight-track machine, in September 1974. Many felt that Traffic's music, whatever the shortcomings on live gigs, was progressing and retained an integrity that many success-conscious bands lacked through working to a formula.

"I think we progressed great," said Jim when we talked in 1989. "'Low Spark Of High Heeled Boys' was a high point. You hear it now and you can't work out if it's rock, jazz, or what. Traffic formed its own style. We used to call it Headless Horsemen music. We really laid the groundwork for lots of other bands who became very technical and scientific. But we kept a very simple approach. Pink Floyd were very close to us in a way, although they were more psychedelic. The Doors had a similar approach. When we played as a trio, with Steve playing the bass pedals on the organ, it felt very free. We were like The Police who made such a brilliant sound with three people. We had organ, drums, and saxophone, and no guitar. Steve would play guitar sometimes, but it was difficult. Chris would have to try and play the organ to back him up. It was difficult to have guitar without a real bass player."

Throughout the life of the group Steve had taken a back seat as far as projecting himself on-stage was concerned. "It was the way he wanted to be," says Jim Capaldi. "That's what makes it so amazing to see him *now!* But when Steve left Spencer to become part of Traffic he was much more serious musically, and it was a big experiment at that time in our lives. It was purely down to the music, no frills, no nothing. It was typical of the period. Things change. It used to be sweaty, amps, leads, trucks . . . that kind of feel. Now it's videos, and getting out there. Steve Winwood today writes very structured songs and he plays them the way they should sound on the record, on-stage. They aren't the sort of songs with an R&B root that you can throw around."

With Traffic finally gone after some six different line-ups, and with the Winwood-Capaldi axis broken, it seemed Steve would at last emerge as a solo performer in his own right. But he seemed to be drained of energy, the years of hard touring had caught up with him. They literally caught up with Chris Wood, who sadly died of liver failure in July 1983 after a long illness.

"Chris was just starting to do his own album at the time of his death," says Nobby Clarke. "He'd been trying to do one for a long while. He died while Steve was out on tour in 1983. We'd just played The Odeon at Hammersmith when we heard he was in hospital and not too well. We were going to go round and see him, then we got a message from his father saying he was a lot better. So we thought we'd finish the shows and then go and see him. Then Chris' father called me and told me he'd passed away. It came as a terrible shock to Steve. Chris had suffered from a liver problem but he actually died from pneumonia."

Chris Wood was more than just a colleague and founder member of Traffic. "I was closer to Chris than anybody," says Steve. "He was probably my very best friend, in many ways." The quiet, gentle and introspective flute and tenor sax player had many notions that appealed to Steve. His ideas about what today would be 'alternative lifestyle' are now usually dismissed as romantic dreams. But in the frantic, materialistic sixties, the first age of consumerism, the yearning for a different, less predictable and uniform life developed fresh and original thinking. Living in a country cottage as a communal band was a start.

Says Steve: "He could be quite a forceful person. We would never plan anything though. We'd just go someplace, then the sun would come up and we'd lie down and go to sleep for a few hours. Then we'd get up and travel on to the next show. Chris was very much responsible for the Traffic 'sound' people recognise. He also brought an element of jazz into the group which gave Traffic something special. I'm very proud of the records we made.

"I did a session with Billy Joel and his guys knew all of the Traffic songs and played them all. His drummer knew every one of Capaldi's fills, and Billy knew all the chords to even the most obscure Traffic songs like 'Withering Tree'. I found it just staggering and it made me realise really what an impact that band had."

Chris Wood was part-writer on many Traffic songs including '40,000 Headmen' and 'Who Knows What Tomorrow May Bring', and their first single 'Paper Sun' featured Chris' distinctive flute sound.

He was trained as an artist and went to the Royal Academy. He stopped painting and decided music was the thing to get into, but the Traffic record covers gave him room for further artistic expression. Steve recalls that Chris shared some of Bob Dylan's ideas about how art and music should be produced. "It was Jeff Lynn (ex-ELO), who told me that in The Travelling Wilburys, whenever anything was too perfect or too nice, Bob Dylan would play something that would just mess it all up. And Chris was into the same kind of thing. If anything was too 'white' he would come up with some little thing to mess it around. He had an unusual talent that was hard to put your finger on. But he was extremely adept and played keyboards and bass on-stage, as well as playing percussion. He could turn his hand to many different instruments including tenor sax and organ. He played bass on songs like 'Pearly Queen'.

"He would never go along with anything because it was easy. He always had something – a style or a sound – he was striving for and never quite reached.

"He wasn't frustrated because he was quite an accomplished musician and so could express himself. He was a quiet person and would never force his will on anyone but he always had specific ideas and was a wonderful conversationalist. He loved to talk to people. Jim is a natural too and would just talk to anybody. He is an outgoing person. Chris wasn't outgoing. Although in a way he *was*. He'd like to talk to people he'd never met before. He would try to strike up acquaintances with people, when he didn't know who they were."

Steve reiterates that Traffic was essentially Jim, Chris and himself. "We were the people who gave the band its character and made that peculiar blend of rock, folk, jazz and R&B. That is what we set out to do in that band, to create a kind of music that is eclectic. It was a conscious effort and Chris was definitely a driving force in Traffic. Jim and I could play and sing, but Chris gave the band its character. Traffic must belong . . . to Chris Wood. He was more responsible for the sound than anyone else."

131

Steve was impressed by Wood's unusual tastes in music and passion for recording. "He would record everything, every note of every jam we played and even conversations, we didn't know he was recording. Then he would play us hours of tape. He would hoard great piles of tapes. He liked everything from Yorkshire folk music to Miles Davis.

"Chris was a victim of everything that happened in rock, but he never bore any malice. In the later days of his life when he got involved in drugs, I didn't see him so much. He was really extraordinary and probably the most fantastic person that I ever knew, and he still influences me in everything I do, and I still like to think that a part of him is with me all the time."

Steve has many happy memories of life on the road with Chris. Like the time Steve decided he didn't want to fly any more and the band went to America by ocean liner. Chris brought along a powerful radio set and picked up all the ship-to-shore messages. "We'd sit in the cabin and listen to everyone's phone calls! There was nothing else to do on the boat, except go to the Over Thirties night!"

What Steve especially liked about Chris Wood was his lack of guile. "There was nothing false or phoney about anything he tried to do. He was absolutely genuine. He did what he felt was good and right."

No one can judge what lures people into addiction to drugs or drink but Chris succumbed to both. "His body couldn't stand up to it," says Steve. "It was a great shame. We all knew he was doing too much and it was difficult to know how to approach it. You can't really sit somebody down and say: 'Let's have a heart to heart talk about this.' Nowadays there is Narcotics Anonymous and if that sort of organisation had existed when Chris was alive – he might still be with us today. They get people who are in the same situation to help, and you can't fool them. Addicts can fool any number of doctors and counsellors, but they use fellow patients to police each other. Chris' death was very sad and a great shock to me."

After the demise of Traffic Steve told *Rolling Stone:* "I'd had enough of this album, tour, album, tour. It was like I was on a treadmill and there was no way of getting off. I just had to say, 'That's it with Traffic; no way can I do it any more.' I wanted to bring discipline to an undisciplined life. I started deliberately mixing with people who had nothing to do with music or any of the arts. There was an idea in the sixties that people who complied to rules or who went to work at nine and came home at five and wore suits, that they were wrong. I suddenly began to realise 'What's wrong with working from nine to five.' I started to do that myself a bit then."

While Steve began the vital process of revitalisation and reorganisation that would eventually banish his old image as the wandering, dreaming raggle-taggle gypsy, Jim Capaldi, too, launched his own career. He went out as a singer, and enjoyed considerable success, starting with 'Oh How We Danced' in 1972 while Traffic were still functioning, followed by 'Short Cut Draw Blood' in 1975 through to 'One Man Mission' in 1984. He released a fine new album in March 1989.

Steve disappeared from the public eye in the years immediately after Traffic's demise. He worked behind the scenes on other peoples' projects. "The demand for Steve was enormous," says Nobby. "We were going up to London all the time trying to fit in sessions." He teamed up or did session work with Viv Stanshall, one-time frontman with The Bonzo Dog Doo Dah Band, with Sandy Denny, Toots And The Maytals, George Harrison, Japanese drummer Stomu Yamashta, Georgie Fame, Marianne Faithfull and The Fania All Stars.

It was a motley crew. He seemed engaged on a musical odyssey that didn't seem to be leading anywhere. But it was regarded by Steve as an important period of education. "It was a conscious attempt to work in as diverse a kind of way as possible. I did get accused of doing nothing but that period when I wasn't doing my own projects was so important in the making of 'Arc Of A Diver'. That really manifested itself later."

For three years Steve was out of the headlines and new names came to dominate the weekly music press. The scene underwent violent change. Said Steve later: "It was a period I needed to go through, so that the pressure on me to work would come only from me again. There's no point in pressure coming from someone else, whether it's an audience or a record company. It doesn't work. Touring was so difficult for me. For every eight months I did it, I'd have to have at least four to recover."

He spent time building his own home studio where he could work at his own tempo and where he could record with Stomu Yamashta's Go. This project included Mike Shrieve, Klaus Schulze, Al

DiMeola, and the ubiquitous Rebop. They produced cosmic music which included Steve's contribution 'Winner/Loser'. Stomu's baby was criticised for being chaotic but it was all part of the learning process Steve then felt he needed. In fact Go encouraged him to attempt his own solo album.

"It suddenly seemed like a good thing. I could have the luxury of working on my own without having to argue. I prefer to work by myself if I can. I sometimes find it difficult to communicate musical ideas," he told Angus MacKinnon. "Before Go I lacked the confidence to make a solo album. I had a lot of material ready but couldn't force myself any further. I couldn't see any real justification for doing it."

This was the period when Steve began to develop his reputation for being a 'recluse' so I was surprised and delighted to see him make a rare appearance at The Lyceum, just off London's Strand, where we'd last seen him with Airforce. He was playing guitar with the current rage, Salsa band The Fania All Stars. He looked and sounded great!

Reviewing the first half of the seventies, Steve now thinks: "They were a bit of a muddle! Looking back on the period of Blind Faith and Airforce, they were a muddle in that I can never remember the chronology of it. But really the whole decade was a bit of a muddle for me, except for Traffic during the Muscle Shoals period and during 'The Low Spark Of High Heeled Boys' and 'When The Eagle Flies' . . . or 'When The Pigeon Drops' as Tom Lord Alge calls it! There were a lot of projects that followed but I didn't quite know where I was going. I wanted to work with as many varied and different types of players as possible. It was during that period I did the album with Stomu Yamashta, and I played on The Fania All Stars album and played with them at The Lyceum. I did endless sessions with people like Richard Thompson and Marianne Faithfull."

Accompanying this turbulent, restless period there came a significant change in Steve's feelings about the whole music business. "I was a bit . . . disappointed. I didn't feel I was taking in enough new information. There was always this pressure of album and tour. I'm not one of these people who can write music on tour. That was the whole idea of having that cottage and spending all that time . . . mucking about! It may have seemed like mucking about, but we were actually making an album. As long as I was on a tour I could never write an album as well. Never could, never will be able to. When I'm doing an album there is no way I can do anything else. I can't have a couple of days off to rehearse a band and still be making an album.

"So I was getting a bit disappointed in the music business and the whole idea of this continuous treadmill. Then I made that album in 1977 which was really, almost an obligation. I was contracted to Island Records and they said: 'Well look, you've really got to put some product out.' I'd been doing sessions and stuff but I hadn't actually been earning any money for that whole period. I'd paid my bills but as far as the record company were concerned, they weren't seeing any income. And of course record companies get very worried, when they don't see that . . ."

So, in 1976, Steve went into the studio to work with a band that included Andy Newmark, Jim Capaldi and guitarist Junior Marvin. They worked hard and then at last in 1977 he produced his first solo album 'Steve Winwood'. One track, 'Midland Maniac', was entirely written, performed, produced and engineered by Steve. He had at last done what I'd been secretly hoping he'd have a bash at since 1964!

"'Midland Maniac' was an attempt to do what I eventually ended up doing on 'Arc Of A Diver'," admitted Steve in 1989.

Released in July 1977, it contained six songs, four by Winwood with Jim Capaldi, one by Steve alone and one by Viv Stanshall. Steve explained that he did 'Midland Maniac' alone simply because he couldn't teach anybody else the song's chord changes and also the lyrics had deep personal significance.

"Although the album was an obligation, I put everything into it," says Steve. "It had some great things about it but it came at a time when punk music was coming out and it didn't relate to that at all. I just confirmed myself as being . . . a dinosaur."

Alas, in the year of The Sex Pistols, all of Winwood's musical values were rejected by a rock establishment only too happy to assimilate the dictates of a few cynical publicists. The album was not a huge commercial success. Steve later described the punk era: "It was against everything that I had been or was to that point. It was against music too. It was anti-establishment. They were really just advanced hippies. I'd been through that in the late sixties and during the seventies I suddenly realised the value of being establishment."

The threat to artists of Steve's quality and background posed by punk was obvious, and he was in danger of being forgotten by press and public. He was quite close to giving up his whole career. He revealed 10 years later: "Because of the experiences I was having through the early seventies, I was almost preparing myself unknowingly to go into some other area. I wasn't desperate, but I was definitely ready to do whatever was necessary. Here I was in 1977 with this album, and punk music was the big rage. The album was pretty good but it wasn't earth shattering.

"I was in a bit of a predicament really, so I thought to myself: 'I've got one last shot. If that doesn't do any good, I'm giving it up.' I had no idea what I was gonna do . . ."

Even now, with success safely secured, Steve finds that period disturbing and upsetting. Indeed it would have been a sad and tragic end to a career that had shown such promise and shone so brightly if he had finished it there and then.

"But I thought: I'm gonna make one last ditch effort, and I'll make sure I do everything so if anything goes wrong with it I would know I was responsible, and hadn't achieved what I wanted to do. So I did 'Arc Of A Diver' and luckily it *did* achieve something. I don't mean luckily for anybody else, I mean luckily for me. Because by that time I didn't have any money! Or so the record company told me."

The 'Steve Winwood' album didn't sell well but by making 'Arc Of A Diver' at home there was no 'studio time' to pay for and no overheads. Winwood began to generate some much needed income. Few people realised that Steve, after being on the road from the age of 15, and having made some of the greatest hits and albums of the golden age of rock music, was broke. He had his home and studio, but there were bills to pay and nothing coming in to pay them – until 'Arc Of A Diver', the album that revitalised his career and reminded fans how much they'd been missing.

He built the studio that gave birth to 'Arc' in a rural setting that was a more elaborate version of the old Berkshire cottage. He bought the 50-acre farm in 1970, and is much amused to read reports that he paid £400,000 for it. In fact the manor house and farm cost a fraction of that amount.

The farm specialised in sheep and beef and Steve ran it with the help of a local farmer. Another rural activity was training dogs and he developed a passion for clay pigeon shooting, sometimes firing 2000 rounds a week, as he won competitions and prizes. It all seemed a far cry from the teenage Winwood who liked nothing better than raving it up in the nightclubs of London. Ten years on he preferred a quiet walk in the countryside. He explained in an interview: "People like myself who have been brought up in towns often move to the country. I'm lucky to be able to live there. If you're prepared to take an active interest in what's going on around you there, you've almost got yourself a full-time occupation. People are a bit suspicious at first, but there's a lot more to it all than jolly people tearing around on horses. I have my dogs, go for walks . . . it's very therapeutic."

"I'm definitely interested in the rural life, although I don't run the farm myself," Steve told the author. "I've always had an arrangement with the neighbours. I've taken a more active part at various times and I'm real good friends with the farmers. I always walk around the farm, although most farmers don't. They go round in a Land Rover. I like to keep up with the price of sheep and stuff but farming today tends to be a lot of playing the Government grants game. It's a tight business. I'm not completely removed from the farm. I do have to go away a lot obviously, but I'm so involved in every aspect of rural life, I'd find it hard not to be here. I love being in Nashville too, although as I say, we don't have a farm in Nashville because we've got one here! Nashville is great for music, it has a lot of rock and soul and R&B. It's just a great place to be. Most of the people in my band now are from Nashville."

It was in 1978 that Steve married his first wife, Nicole Tacot from Los Angeles, whom he'd met through Chris Wood's wife. The marriage was not a success, and became the source of some anguish for Steve. There were many conflicting versions of the reasons for its failure. It was claimed that Nicole became immersed in the English country lifestyle . . . and didn't enjoy big city life. In fact the opposite was true.

Says Winwood heatedly: "I read some incredible stuff in the press in which they painted a picture of her being this country person. It was absolute *rubbish!* She hated the country. She *hated* it. She used to spend all her time in London. I was the one who loved the country, and used to play organ in the church and make friends with the neighbours – she didn't get on with them at all."

The cause, it seems, was Nicole's abrasive tones. "She was rude to the neighbours and she was rude to my parents. She was rude to everybody." Eventually Nicole moved out of Steve's manor house and lived in a flat in London. It was a depressing burden for Steve to suffer at a time when as far as his career and personal happiness was concerned, he needed all the help and support he could get.

He talks quietly but with controlled passion about that fraught period in his life. One night the author and Steve sat in the quiet backroom of a rural pub, The Plough, not far from his home. There we drank real ale, Steve sitting next to the pub's upright piano that would remain untouched, as he described the background to his first marriage.

"She got a flat when we were supposedly married. The marriage was never a good marriage at all. It was like we led separate lives and in the end, we slept in separate beds." For the last period of their marriage they had separate rooms, and it was obviously not a situation that could be allowed to last.

"I must confess I probably stayed with it for convenience, for a long time which was the wrong thing to do. I had met her through Chris Wood's wife Jeanette. But it was not a comfortable marriage, it was very rocky. And all that stuff about her wanting to stay in the country wasn't true. She had this flat in London and I hardly went there. She had a lot of friends there who I didn't know.

"I kept the marriage going because I didn't want to go through the inconvenience of a divorce. I kept it going for much longer than I should have done. I have never told my side of the story, and all this stuff got out in the press about how she loved the country and that was ridiculous. When I was in America, she wasn't spending a lot of time in the country, she was off to London."

It was a strain but he wouldn't let it affect his work. "I just used to escape to the studio. I had country friends who would drive by to see if her car was there, and if it wasn't then all my mates would come in. And then when she came back, they'd all get going, and I would escape too and get on with my work."

Many of Steve's songs from this period sound sorrowful and he agrees he may have been influenced by what was going on in his private life.

"Yes, maybe. It was a troubled period. I tried to just ignore it. Maybe I thought it would just go away if I ignored it. Yeah, I was influenced by it but particularly on 'Arc Of A Diver' I was singing the songs other people had written. I did the music but really they were about things other people were going through. Lines like 'She bathed me in sweetness', was Viv Stanshall's. Viv and I knew each other and spent a lot of time doing stuff, but that was what *he* was thinking. Songs I did with Will Jennings didn't really have to do with any personal relationship. That's why it worked.

"With 'While You See A Chance', you don't have to feel up or down. That's just a fact. He was writing about things other than personal relationships and that's why it did so well. Will is like a script writer. He looks at people and has the knack of knowing what will suit them. But with that song, he wasn't sending me messages. If he had anything to say to me he'd sit me down in a pub and say: 'Listen mate, if I were you I'd get out of there and do something else.' He wasn't sending me subtle hints with that song. He just felt it was the right kind of positive song I should be doing after a lot of doomy, gloomy stuff I'd done in the seventies and early eighties. He saw me in this new light, and I saw myself in that light too.

"Will said that the first time he'd met me he didn't know what to expect. He hadn't really been a big Traffic fan, so he looked me up in the *Rolling Stone History Of Rock*, and they said . . . 'Winwood is a victim of the drugs he ushered in, in the seventies.' That's what they said. Which was nice of them. It wasn't true, but he expected me to be a real druggie person. I've never been that really. We used to smoke a lot of pot, and I used to have a few drinks, but I've never really been into serious drugs as have a few of my contemporaries, as they have admitted. I really haven't been involved in any serious drug taking at all. Yeah, I did take some acid in the sixties – but not for long! And I had to stop smoking pot. I can't do that any more. It just doesn't agree with me. I haven't smoked anything in 10 years."

137

while you see a chance

Steve Winwood has never worked in splendid isolation. Partnerships and team work have always been important to him. From the earliest days of his career he has had people around able to help, advise or form a musical framework. One of his oldest associates is Jim Capaldi, but after the heyday of Traffic they began to drift apart.

Steve and Jim had worked together on the 'Steve Winwood' album but says Jim: "After that I went off to Brazil and we kind of split up then because I was so far away, and much to my regret, Will Jennings came in as his co-composer and between them they did four, five, six million-selling albums! I didn't write one song on them! Maybe I'll put that right now. Will Jennings came from the Midwest, Nashville way. He's a very good lyricist."

Another partner in songwriting was Viv Stanshall, the creative genius behind the much loved Bonzo Dog Doo Dah Band, an ex-art school creation that mixed surrealist or Da Da humour with musical pastiche. They achieved considerable commercial success in the sixties and became an integral part of the rock scene before they burnt themselves out. Vivian, who had been the Bonzo's frontman and lyricist, was adept at word-play and came up with the title 'Arc Of A Diver', which he co-wrote.

"That album was a big, big turning point for me," says Steve. "It gave me a direction in music and gave me some confidence in my own work. It gave me the means to continue, and it was also a combination of everything that I had learned during those seventies years when I had been working on everybody else's albums. Also that was a period when I was learning about recording and about the way different people work. I did learn a bit about studio techniques in Traffic and in fact there is a song on 'John Barleycorn Must Die' where I played everything, which was 'A Stranger To Himself'. Jim sang on it and played some percussion but I played drums, piano and guitar. So I guess I was starting to learn from the seventies onwards and from working on other people's projects.

"This culminated in 'Arc Of The Diver' when I put together everything I knew plus a little I didn't! Somehow it seemed to work and I was very lucky."

It was the first album that Steve wrote mostly with Will Jennings. Says Steve of his new co-writer: "I learned about discipline from Will. When we wrote 'While You See A Chance' (his optimistic 1981 US Top Ten hit) we didn't talk about what the song was about. He just came up with this lyric and it was right for me, right for him and right for the song.

"That song got a Million Play award (in 1988), which was my first ever. It's very difficult to get especially at the age of forty! They say that if you play a three-minute song on the radio a million times that represents five years! It means that at various times that song was playing on different radio stations around the world at the same time which is amazing. Whilst it's wonderful to be voted Best Keyboard Player or Brightest Hope, those kind of awards are very nice, but having a Million Play is one of the best you can get. No one voted for that because they think you are a nice bloke or whatever. They just played the record and for me that is a great thing."

Will and Steve would go on to write all the songs on 'Talking Back To The Night' and most of 'Back In The High Life' and 'Roll With It'. "We do work quite closely together. We started off with him doing the lyrics and me the music and that was it. Now we discuss things more closely together than we did in the early days. Will plays guitar, but he doesn't play when we write together."

Oddly enough, despite Steve's subsequent success with hit albums and singles, Jim Capaldi still feels that Steve's pioneering work with The Spencer Davis Group remains some of his best. "I was playing a compilation tape of the old group in the car the other day and flashed back on just how brilliant Steve was in those days. He did things then he'll never top because he was unashamedly going for R&B soul, and he had the chops, and the voice, and the playing was just faultless. He sounded older then . . . he sounds younger now! Then he sounded as if he had been on the blues circuit for years and had come off the back porch down south. The feel was so authentic. He still has to be the premier musician and singer from England. It's interesting that with Phil Collins and Peter Gabriel coming through, they say Steve sounds like them. That's because they've suddenly had huge success, whereas, after Traffic, Steve took a big break. The newer generation just don't realise that they *all* grew up on Steve!"

Steve wasn't ready to be part of history, or to accept that his best work was behind him. For Steve, the mid-eighties would see him flower in a way that astonished his friends and contemporaries. But there was a hiccup. 'Talking Back To The Night', released by Island in a somewhat garish yellow sleeve in the summer of 1982, was not quite as successful as he'd hoped. Steve had done much promotion for 'Arc', going on tours in Europe and America and, unusually for him, doing many press and radio interviews.

"I went to the warehouses and shook hands with all the guys shipping out the records and all that kind of stuff. Then I thought: 'Right, I know how to make these solo albums! I've finally got it.' Two years later I went back in and did this 'Talking Back To The Night', and it stiffed completely!" Steve laughs ruefully.

"That happened really because . . . well I'm not making excuses. Albums stiff because they don't sell. And it didn't sell because it wasn't really that good."

Steve has some theories about music and its intimate relation-ship with commerce. "I don't think the market place is the absolute end in terms of musical importance. Because something sells that doesn't mean it's gotta be good and if it doesn't sell it's gotta be bad. Having said that – you can't have something you think is brilliant that nobody else likes. I think the reason there is such a schism between classical and rock music now is because classical music is subsidised. Orchestras can't make a profit, and I think their concession to the market place, like the London Symphony Orchestra playing The Beatles, is off really. I think that's a bit duff. It's the wrong way to go and that's a real problem. They play 100-year-old classical music, but 100 years ago they didn't. They played the music of *now*, the current music of the day. Anyway, that's just a bee in my bonnet."

Steve smiled as we sat on a bench in the garden, in the summer sunshine, discussing these vexed issues while a man with a chainsaw busily hacked up logs in the distance. Admitting that 'Talking Back To The Night' wasn't a brilliant album, it contained 'Valerie' a solid hit song, though there were lesser songs like 'While There's A Candle Burning' which lacked impact. The album was also put together while a huge technological revolution was going on in pop music at large.

"Technology suddenly leapt in 1981-82," says Steve. "In fact it has developed incredibly in the last 10 years. I spent a lot of time in the seventies working with all those people, you know, playing salsa, which comes from South America, and watching other people working in the studios. The technology boom came later." Steve was fascinated by the arrival of drum machines, sequencers and more sophisticated synthesisers.

"In 1982, after 'Arc Of A Diver' I met Roger Linn creator of the Linn drum, and he showed us what this thing could do and how wonderful it was and then he said, 'Of course it's only really meant for demos.' Which is incredible really because look what happened to his drum machine. Every single hit used it, virtually.

"In fact I'd used a lot of new technology on 'Arc Of A Diver' and thought I'd got it. Yet 'Talking Back To The Night' ended up sounding very under-produced."

Nobby Clarke assisted Steve on the making of 'Arc Of A Diver' and 'Talking Back To The Night'. "It was fantastic," he says. "We were told things were impossible because the technology didn't exist. There were no sophisticated drum machines and no codes to synchronise stuff. If you wanted to move bits around it could take hours and hours. This was all pre-digital technology. Digital wasn't even a concept at that time. It was just being developed when we did 'Talking Back To The Night' and programmable drum machines came in.

"In fact, Steve played all the drums on those records. We made drum loops but he did all the playing, and every single thing you hear on 'Arc Of A Diver' is Steve, from the artistic point of view Steve engineered all the record. I just did the technical stuff and made sure it got on to tape. It took more than two years to make. The record company thought Steve had gone crazy! It was unheard of for one person to play everything on a record. It didn't seem possible in those days but he was determined, and it was just a question of finding a way of doing everything.

"It was a huge experiment and one that worked well. The master of 'Spanish Dancer' is only one minute and 10 seconds long, which is why when you listen to it carefully you hear some of the vocals are a little distorted. That recording is the very first time he sang those lyrics. We'd used up all the tracks and we sat there and thought, 'Shall we try and recut the vocals?' But the performance was so good we decided not to. If it was distorted it didn't matter."

Steve used a Mini Moog to create the distinctive solo on 'While You See A Chance' and Nobby explains how the famous introduction came on to the song. "There was a slight accident in the studio when I erased all the drum tracks! We had a custom-built remote control panel on the side of the recording desk. I had all the lyric sheets resting on there. We put the vocal track on and Steve said, 'I'm not hearing the drums.' I hit the stop button and lifted all these papers up. They had pushed all the drum tracks in 'Record'. We spent a couple of weeks trying to get the drums back but we couldn't get the drums to match. Then we were listening to the tape-back and Steve found that bit of Moog which he had played right at the end of the song. He recognised it instantly as being the perfect way to open the song. We cut it up, put it at the beginning and it meant we didn't need the drums any more. It worked perfectly. The disaster turned into something really memorable. It had been a terrible two weeks trying to patch things up and we ended up with pure magic."

Steve didn't feel isolated working on his own in this way. Says Nobby: "He thinks it's much easier working with less people. In the old days we had to get three or four people all together and try and get them to play right at the same time."

Many early Traffic albums do sound pretty rough in comparison to Steve's modern recordings and, says Clarke: "Well, that's the way they were recording . . . as a band. You get to the point where you say, 'This is an incredible performance but do we scrap it because somebody is out of tune?' Hopefully these days when a band records, everybody, including the engineer, gets it right at the same time. Traffic might record a great track and then not like the sound. An engineer is an integral part of the band and he needs to get it right too."

For the compilation album 'Chronicles' Steve and engineer Tom Lord Alge remixed 'Valerie'. They carefully put on a better drum sound and more echo and the result appealed to radio audiences in particular. 'Chronicles' became a million-seller in the States.

"I try to use technology and not abuse it," says Steve. "I'll use it in any way and I'm not prejudiced about it. There are some people who say look what great records they made before drum machines or synthesisers. That's fine. Nothing wrong with that, but personally I'm *so* interested in the technology I like to use it. On 'Roll With It' I did nearly all the programming. There's a lot more on it than you'd think. For example we used a mixture of real drums and some triggered from a machine. Russ Kunkel is great at playing real drums along with machines."

Steve fears he lost a lot of old fans by using new techniques on his records, but they must have been pretty much die-hard stick-in-the-muds not to appreciate the vast improvements made in every department from tuning to time keeping to sheer sound quality.

"I think those people will come round even now, in the late eighties. People have realised you don't have to be 17 to enjoying listening to music. But when I did 'Arc Of A Diver' a lot of people tried to compare it to my early records from Spencer Davis to Traffic."

143

When 'Talking Back To The Night' was a flop on release in America, its failure was a shock. "I had to have another re-think," says Steve. "It made me want to give in." He seriously considered giving up making records himself and becoming a producer. But in the end the encouragement and advice he needed came from a source that had helped him since childhood – his brother Muff.

"Muff convinced me that I should carry on with my artist's career, instead of just going into production." Muff told Steve: "Look, you're 37 now. If you produce now for four years, and then decide you wanna make another solo album, you'll be 42 and it will be much more difficult for you."

Steve took heart and responded immediately to his brother's advice. "It's funny, in an old interview with you, I said about Muff that we always disagree and he's always right. It's true even now. We still disagree, but I'm closer to Muff now than I've ever been. I wasn't very close to him in The Spencer Davis Group, which is what I said to you 20 years ago, but we were just on top of each other in the confines of the group, and since those days we've got really close. He's signed some amazing talent to CBS, from Adam Ant to Bros and Terence Trent Darby. I don't always agree with him but he's often right! He gave me good advice about my career, and at that point I did go out and work with all those musicians in the States.

"I went out and got a new manager, I got a producer, and I went to New York and did the album 'Back In The High Life'. I'd been to New York before in 1982 and had been there for quite a long time. I lived there on my own for a few months while I was auditioning that first band I toured with in '83, and I started to like New York more."

It was the first time Steve was able to get a feel of the city streets and its shops and apartments, offices and studios, and not just be rushed around from door to door in a limo. It was actually the first time he'd been to the States in 10 years. He met producer Russ Titelman who listened to Steve's demos. "I started staying at his house where he lived two hours outside New York. But I said to Russ: 'Forget it, I want to live in the City.' There were all these fantastic people playing at The Village Voice each night. It was just wonderful to see people like Bo Diddley or David 'Fathead' Newman, who had played with Ray Charles."

Steve first met Titelman when he was recording with George Harrison at the ex-Beatle's Henley home. Russ was producing Harrison and Steve played keyboards and did backing vocals for George. Russ also produced a Christine McVie album for which Steve wrote a song. Steve then invited Russ to co-produce 'Back In The High Life'.

While in New York Steve would go to watch the Mel Lewis Big Band on Monday nights, and was knocked out to renew his acquaintance with live jazz. "It was great! I fell in love with New York. It's a real 24-

hour city with traffic jams at five am. I'd often walk from my apartment to the studio, or from mid-town to Greenwich Village."

"When Steve was back in New York to record 'Back In The High Life' he went to The Power Station studio and then decided to go to Unique Studio to use a room called Midi City," says Nobby Clarke. "Steve was supposed to have worked with Chris Lord Alge, Tom's older brother. He couldn't make the session so Tom did it and Steve really liked him because he was brought up on computers and new technology. Tom has done every single session since. I don't work in the studio with Steve any more although I help set the stuff up. I just don't have the time to sit there for hours."

It was in New York that Steve found a new manager. "I'd really never had a manager before," he says. Most people assumed that Chris Blackwell, his mentor since 1964, had been his manager, but as he owned the record company Steve was signed to, it was felt there was a 'conflict of interest', and says Steve: "I think he realised that at some point and ceased to be my manager."

His new manager is Los Angeles based Ron Weisner who has worked with Michael Jackson and Madonna. It was Weisner who made sure 'Back In The High Life' wouldn't be another home studio job. He would get him out of cosy Gloucestershire and back to the States. Weisner told *Rolling Stone:* "I told Steve: 'When I saw you in the past, I never knew if you had legs.' Because you would never see him up. He would be very laid-back and timid."

With a six-piece band Winwood went back on the road in 1983, visiting Europe and Britain, and received a hero's welcome. Steve at last stepped out from behind the defensive wall of keyboards, and became a charming, communicative entertainer – without overdoing things. He talked, made announcements and banished memories of the bashful youth of yore. Not that his new generation of fans knew or cared about times past. Steve was very much making hits for the day.

"It was the first time he'd gone out and hired a complete band," says Nobby. "Steve auditioned people in New York, then went out on the road. Audiences hadn't changed and fundamentally everything seemed pretty much the same. But it has changed in the last few years. Technology has arrived in a big way, to the point where it takes a long time to set up. We need two productions that leap frog each other, and Steve's audiences now, particularly in America, have an enormous age span. When we did the 'Back In The High Life' tour audiences were aged from mid-twenties to thirty whereas on the 'Roll With It' world tour there were many more young people, which was great.

"Steve still loves playing but he doesn't like the physical part of touring," says Clarke. "He enjoys playing now as much as he ever did. His voice may have been stronger in the early days but it wasn't looked

145

after. Now he takes more care of it and he's singing a lot better. I couldn't be more pleased for him. I think he deserved his recent success because he's an incredibly talented person."

Winwood had decided to take charge of his destiny with a determination and vigour that surprised everyone. "I made a conscious effort to start working with musicians and producers and engineers."

Steve talked to me about his decision to go back to touring. "It was '83 I went back to touring to promote the album. It was a bit daunting but quite exciting because a lot of things had changed about being on-stage. I hadn't done it for 10 years. I'd done odd things, but not a tour. It was great – I don't know if I chose the right band at that stage. But the band I have now is absolutely fantastic. And a great bunch of people."

He went to New York in July 1985 to start work on 'Back In The High Life' which was released in July 1986. He broke from his previous pattern of recording virtually everything himself and recruited Joe Walsh, Chaka Khan, Nile Rodgers, James Ingram and James Taylor and the result was one of his most sophisticated and successful albums. Joe Walsh co-wrote one of the tracks, 'Split Decision', on which he played guitar. The album was nominated for six Grammy Awards in 1986, the most of any artist that year, and won three. They were Record Of The Year and Best Pop Male Vocal Performance for 'Higher Love' and Best Engineered Recording. 'Higher Love' was Steve's first number one hit single in America and was long overdue recognition but it was none the less welcome.

"The album was very successful," says Steve. "And after that we had 'Chronicles' when Island were kind enough to allow me to choose what went on it and re-mix it. It was a compilation of my solo work and we re-mixed some of the 'Talking Back' stuff. That did extremely well and 'Valerie' was a big hit."

It was during his return to the States that he met Eugenia Crafton at a Junior Walker show in New York in 1985. It was a chance meeting that would bring tremendous change and great happiness to both their lives. Steve would eventually divorce Nicole in December 1986, and marry Eugenia on January 17, 1987, in a New York church. Genia gave birth to their daughter, Mary Clare, on May 20 in a Nashville hospital.

Says Steve: "It seems to some people that I got divorced one month and married the next, but what was overlooked was that my marriage had deteriorated over a long, long time and the divorce dragged on and on because of all the financial aspects."

Eugenia is the great love in Steve's life. She is charming, beautiful and has brought him companionship, support, understanding and two lovely children. In return Steve has proved to be caring, considerate and the kind of gentleman that girls from the South most appreciate. They might seem worlds apart; he an English musician brought up in the vast urban sprawl of Birmingham, she a small-town doctor's daughter, not long out of college. In fact they have much in common. Certainly, the chemistry that brought them together has seen a blossoming of shared delights and interests. Both have an easy, relaxed manner balanced by an inner firmness. They make decisions together but they refrain from interfering with matters that specially concern either one. Eugenia would never dream of advising Steve on his music, but she'll take care that his public image suits him. Likewise Steve gives Genia free rein in choosing the furnishings and decor of the ancient manor house they now share together.

Since coming to live in England Genia has taken care to avoid becoming an American 'Lady of the Manor', and can sink a pint of real ale in the village inn with a gusto to match Steve's. They are both fond of dogs, and Genia loves horses, although Steve tends to regard the latter with some suspicion, ever since he was kicked in the elbow by a horse. That was back in 1978 and for nine months, while his broken right arm was on the mend, there was some fear whether he'd be able to play again. But eventually the vital radial movement was restored. He's since formed the opinion that, like human beings, horses are unpredictable beasts.

Genia however loves to ride, and was leading her horse back to the manor house at the end of a hot June day when the author called to talk about her life with Steve.

Steve and Genia met in 1985, and Genia came to England with Steve the following May. She graduated from college in December 1987, with a degree in Business Administration. Her ambition, before she met Steve, was to get a job in sales and marketing. For a while she had unpaid work experience at Warner Brothers, where she telephoned radio stations and helped set up displays in Nashville record stores.

Eugenia was born in Trenton, Tennessee, a town with a population of around 4,000, most of them farm workers. "It was a very small place and you knew everybody in town," she recalls. Her father was a physician who helped found the local hospital. "He was a country doctor who made house calls all his life," says Genia. Her parents had three children and Genia has an older brother and sister. Her father died in 1980. She has fond memories of the happy times she had growing up with her family. "It was a beautiful town with houses with porches that wrapped around, where everyone sat out. All my family lived on one block. Our home was in between my grandmother's and my aunt's. All my cousins were close by."

She went to elementary school in Trenton, then later her parents sent her to a boarding school, Swanee Academy, in Tennessee. She graduated and went to college in Knoxville.

"I really didn't know what I wanted to study, but I kinda had the experience of going to a very big college which was a lot of fun. I left because my grade point average was slowly dropping!" After leaving, Eugenia went to Nashville where she obtained a cosmotology licence which enabled her to do hair dressing. "But I knew I didn't want to do that forever." She rented her own premises which got her interested in business. "I then knew what I wanted to study, so I went back to college."

Genia met Steve Winwood while she was still in college. She had never been to New York City and when a few friends decided to make a weekend trip to the Big Apple, they invited her along. They stayed with a girlfriend, as they couldn't afford a hotel. "We just slept on the floor," she recalls. The friends decided to visit The Lone Star Café to see Junior Walker And The All Stars. The alto sax player was one of the stars of Tamla Motown in the sixties, and his band's rocking instrumental, 'Shotgun' had been a Top 10 hit in 1965. The sound of Junior's wailing sax and the band's funky, driving beat was an irresistible magnet to anyone with an affinity for soul and R&B.

"I was, and still am, a big fan of his," says Genia. She was sitting at a table in The Lone Star when in walked a group of people. "It was Steve and some of his buddies. He had evidently been working in the studio and had taken a break to come and see Junior Walker. He sat at a table beside us, but I didn't actually notice him. My friends did – but I was standing on a chair watching the band and having a good time!"

Genia's friend Marty called out, "Hey, this is Steve Winwood!" Genia smiled a greeting and said "Hi Steve," and the two parties merged in their enthusiasm for the band's stomping performance. As the last blasting notes reverberated around The Lone Star, Steve said, "We're all going to The China Club now, why don't you all join us?"

Steve got to the China before Eugenia and her friends, who found the new place even more crowded than The Lone Star. But the two groups made their way on to the dance floor, where some complicated negotiations were put in motion. Steve asked one of his friends to ask one of Genia's friends whether Genia would like to dance with Steve. There was whispered shuttle diplomacy. They danced. They fell in love.

"Steve told a friend he was interested in me and later we sat and talked and he asked if he could have my phone number," says Genia. "I remember we all got his autograph that night. I thought he must have been interested because on everybody else's autograph he wrote 'Regards from Steve Winwood', and on mine he wrote 'Love from Steve Winwood'. I thought . . . mmm!"

Genia gave Steve her number and she went back to her friend's house. Steve called the next morning, and asked her if she'd like to go out to dinner. They went out and talked, and talked. It was love at first sight. Says Genia: "Well, it seems that way. If it wasn't it was soon after. All the men in my family have been outdoors types, into shooting and hunting, and so we talked a lot about that, and he realised I was a country girl. And Steve had really got into country life, during the time when people didn't see much of him. So we had that in common."

Steve took Genia out every night during her subsequent stay in New York. After that he would visit her in Nashville every weekend or she would fly to see him, while he was working on 'Back In The Highlife'. Genia found the whole experience tremendously exciting. "It was real fun for me, although Steve was going through his divorce at that time. He and I both thought that he really had to take care of that before things could get serious, and I was also in a very deep relationship with a fella, but it wasn't working out that well. So that was almost like a divorce too. We kinda had to straighten out our own situations before we could commit to each other. We just kept in touch and talked every day. It wasn't something that we just *jumped* into. We were friends who talked and really got to know each other. Steve was wonderful. He took me to so many places while we were dating."

They kept the relationship going on this level from September until May the following year when Eugenia came to England with Steve for the first time. She stayed at his home for five weeks, and recalls: "That's when we finally decided we just wanted to see each other and didn't want to date anybody else."

Genia and Steve travelled directly from the airport to the Cotswolds and Genia immediately fell in love with the house and its setting. "We took long walks every day with the dogs, and I just got to see his home and know about the way he lived in his own environment, because he had been to Tennessee and seen mine. I fell in love with it."

There were similarities between Gloucestershire and Tennessee in the landscape of rolling hills, although England is much greener and lusher. Genia found people tended to be more reserved too.

"English people have a different personality . . . they are more open in Tennessee, and they'll talk to you more, even if they don't know you. But everyone was pleasant to me in England and the neighbours made me feel really welcome. Steve had a party when I first arrived so I could meet all his friends. They were really nice and we stayed up until the wee hours dancing and having a good time here at the house."

In fact the first time Steve and Eugenia met they stayed up all night talking. Their past lives merged as they exchanged their experiences and feelings and shared their thoughts, a pattern that would continue at every meeting.

"I thought that was really special, to be able to do that. And when I came to England we just got into Steve's Dino Ferrari and took rides through the countryside and talked as we drove. Steve is a gentleman, and he has the nicest manners. He's so thoughtful and considerate."

149

As they got to know each other over the weeks following their first meeting, Steve and Genia found they both liked to go to church. "We began to go to church together when we started dating in New York and that was really nice. He loved his mum and dad too, and I thought that was very important. And he was just so nice to me and seemed to love me so much . . . and I'd never been loved like that. I'd never been treated that special way. I was pretty mixed up in the other relationship I had and Steve taught me a lot about love and what true love really is."

It was Steve Winwood the man and not the famous celebrity Genia met and grew to love. His personality and character made a deep impression on her. "But that of course is besides his being an incredibly talented musician. I'd been aware of his famous songs like 'Gimme Some Lovin'' and 'I'm A Man', but I hadn't bought Spencer Davis albums. I did have Traffic LPs and a couple of solo albums, but you know, I could have sat all night long next to him and not known it was Steve Winwood. I didn't really know what he looked like – I just knew his music!

Word soon spread of the growing affair and Genia laughs: "One of my friends happens to have the biggest mouth in Tennessee! So it was all over Nashville, but I told my sister and my mother that I had met a really nice guy and his name was Steve Winwood. Then he came and met my family."

After Genia's visit to Gloucestershire, the couple went back to New York where they visited one of their favourite spots, The Manhattan Brewery. There took place a romantic interlude.

"As we came out of The Manhattan Brewery he got on his knees on the sidewalk and asked me to marry him! I said, 'Steve, you're drunk, get up. You don't mean it.' And he said 'I do'."

The couple hugged, a friend took a photograph and the pair got into a cab. There were still problems to consider however. Eugenia was still at college and Steve's divorce wasn't finalised. So there were no marriage plans made and they held off from talking any more about the idea.

"Steve had a tour to do, and then . . . I got pregnant. It was in August, and then Steve gave me an engagement ring in October. I didn't want to get married while Steve was on tour, and I was studying for exams." Genia graduated from college in December and the couple got married in January.

The wedding took place at the Fifth Avenue Presbyterian Church. "It was just perfect . . . really everything we both wanted. It was a very small wedding with only our immediate family and just a few friends. The church was the one we had always gone to on Sundays in New York. We invited my preacher from Tennessee who helped in the service with the preacher from Fifth Avenue."

Genia's family flew from Nashville while Steve's family arrived from England on Concorde, including his mother and father, brother Muff and his wife, and his niece and nephew. Limousines were laid on for the weekend and the guests were taken to see a Broadway show, appropriately, *Me And My Girl*.

The wedding ceremony took place at three in the afternoon and Genia was crying so hard from emotion that Steve grew quite alarmed. "Steve said later he wondered whether I'd changed my mind! He was teasing. I just felt I was getting the sweetest man in the world . . . and I still believe that."

After the service came an intimate reception followed by the couple's two-month honeymoon on the Caribbean island of St. Barts where they rented a house. It seemed like a long time away but, for tax reasons, Steve couldn't live in either Britain or America for a while. "Steve was doing his 'year off'" explains Genia. "But the island was a real paradise, an old French colony. I made the decisions for each day – where to eat and which beach to go to. There were some beautiful restaurants there and we had lovely picnics too." The idyll was broken only by a flight to New York for the Grammy Awards. They went back to St. Barts for a further stay and then . . . their first baby was born in May.

"Steve was wonderful. He came into the delivery room and was really nervous. But it couldn't have been any easier and there were no problems at all. She was as healthy as could be and weighed 8lbs.13ozs. We never found out whether we had a boy or a girl before she was born, and we were just really pleased at having a daughter." The name Mary Clare was chosen because of the Southern tradition of using double names. Steve's mother's middle name was Mary, and Clare was a name that appealed to Genia.

"Other names came up but we always came back to Mary Clare. There is 18 months difference between the two girls. By the time we had Elizabeth Dawn, Steve was getting to be quite a pro in the delivery room, and he cut the cord. As a matter of fact the doctor was telling him a joke in the delivery room and I called out, 'You all come *here!*'" They rushed to put their gloves on and Steve cut the umbilical cord.

The life of a rock musician, for all its transient moments of glory, its promises of easy fame and riches, can be a hollow, disappointing and often meaningless existence. Many who were caught up in the music boom of the sixties, and lived their lives according to the dictates of its fashions and philosophies, found, in the end, only despair and darkness. "I have looked into the pit," one of rock's most famous clowns told the author one night. It was a remark that seemed far fetched and melodramatic. A year later, Keith Moon was found dead, a victim of the senseless pursuit of the unobtainable high.

151

What makes the turn of events in Steve's career so heartwarming is that when he cut the superficialities of the music business from his life, he enriched it with family life and strong beliefs. But he did it all without loud trumpetings of some ephemeral cult. At the same time he was able to encapsulate his lifetime's musical experience into a presentation that would appeal to a hugely expanded audience.

His personality blossomed with his career, in a way that has already been noted and commented on by friends and colleagues. How much of that wave of change was triggered by his marriage to Eugenia only she and Steve can say.

Eugenia is careful not to claim too much credit. "I think marriage has made him comfortable enough to work and think freely. He can relax and do his best work. Obviously I never knew Steve in the days of his previous marriage but people do tell me he has changed. He has come out of himself so much more. This is what his friends tell me and I think he is really happy. I hope he is.

"He's a wonderful father. He gets up early and takes the kids downstairs and lets me lie in while he gets the breakfast. That's usually our routine. We'll get up and get the children fed and then take a stroll with them. Then the nanny comes at 10 am and we get them back at around five in the afternoon. I love to cook, so I'll cook supper, and then after supper, we'll give them a bath, read a story and put them to bed."

Having a big house to look after, even with the help of a nanny, was rather daunting for Genia when she first arrived. "He had been married before and his first wife lived here and I didn't know if I would feel comfortable. In fact Steve said, 'Look we'll sell the house.' But I said 'No, it's a beautiful home and I love it. I wanna stay here.' So I redecorated the house and now I do feel it's home for me. And we do have a housekeeper – I thought I would treat myself to that!"

But Genia wasn't just marrying a country gentleman, she was now the wife of one of the most in-demand rock performers and recording artists of the eighties. She would now share with Steve the traumas that sometimes entailed.

"The first time I saw him on-stage I cried, I was so proud of him. I was a nervous wreck! It was almost as if I were gonna be performing. Steve is a real professional. He doesn't take things in a lighthearted way. When he starts a tour for the first few shows he's always pretty nervous.

"The band are nervous too. Steve never allows his band to take drugs or drink – certainly not before a show. That's one thing he doesn't allow, and the musicians are very serious about their work too. But by the end of a tour they are much more relaxed and will say: 'Well, guess we gotta go on in five minutes . . .' there's a big difference to the atmosphere.

But every time I hear Steve's voice it brings a lump in my throat. I think it's beautiful. He has such *soul* about him."

When Steve later recorded 'Roll With It' in Dublin, Genia went with him to the sessions. "I found 'Back In The Highhlife' a lot more fun because it was done in New York which is more exciting, but Dublin was an interesting city for me. I'm not one to sit around the studio. I like to be busy and don't want to be in the way. I would go out and hear some other bands while he worked, and then meet him afterwards and have some Guinness!"

Genia admits she couldn't cope with the kind of intensive touring that many rock musicians endure, often going out on the road for two years at a stretch. "Steve's tours don't last more than three months. He's ready to stop by that point. I don't know if I could cope with much over that. I like him at home! And he likes to be at home. But touring is exciting and it helps to please his fans because I know if it weren't for his fans, we wouldn't have the lifestyle we have, we wouldn't be able to enjoy a lot of the things we have, so if he has to give back something to the people who have bought his records, a part of him, then that's fine and I'm willing to share that part."

Eugenia doesn't lay claim to coming from a musical family like Steve, but she can play piano – by ear. "I've always loved music and bought albums, and I love to dance. I've got music in me but I don't have a good voice. We have a piano in the dining room but I'm not a great player. All I can say is I have a good ear for music. Steve and I sing together all the time. We like a lot of the same artists, and tend to go back to that Memphis music a lot."

Genia wouldn't presume to influence Steve's work when writing or recording but she shares with him a concern about his image when it comes to making promotional videos. "I don't know if it's the record companies or the directors, but so many times Steve and I look at a video and send it back. They try to make him come off as some kind of sex object or something, and I don't think you have to be that to sell albums. I think videos should be interesting but you have to be very careful because he is married and has children. You have to decide what image you want to have and stick with it, because if you're not careful the directors can get carried away. I mean – he is handsome – but you have to be careful. We always look at the videos together and talk about everything, and we make decisions together. Lots of times people think we are being too picky but it's what we believe and I think it has paid off to be that way."

Genia put her business studies to good use when she met Steve. Over the years he never had to book air tickets, take care of accounts or any other management details. He had always had other people taking care of business for him since his teens. Now he wanted to learn and Genia was able to help.

153

"When we first met Steve told me he wanted to learn to do these things. He never had – being who he is. Other people did it for him. Now I do things like paying bills. It's just the sort of thing that everybody in the world normally has to do, but Steve didn't. Even things like carrying his own bags to the car. He's kinda come back to reality a little bit."

It would be too much to expect even with a happy marriage like Steve and Genia's that absolutely everything would be perfect. Not long after they were married there were press reports that Genia was trying to force Steve to do things her way. "The thing that upset me when we got married was when the English papers said I was going to sell Steve's house, and that just wasn't true. Because I was new to the situation it upset me more than it would now.

"I just realised the papers are always going to say things that aren't true and you just don't let it bother you. It was made to look as though I had come into his life and taken him away and that wasn't how it was at all!"

Above: Steve rehearsing for the orchestral performance of Pete Townshend's *Tommy* at London's Rainbow Theatre, 1973. *(Barry Plummer)*

Above: Steve performing with Traffic at their final appearance at the Reading Festival, August 1974. *(Barry Plummer)*

Above: Jim Capaldi and Steve on-stage with Traffic. *(Barry Plummer)*

Above: Blind Faith 'rehearsing' at Eric Clapton's Surrey home in 1969. Left to right: Steve, Ric Grech, Ginger Baker and Eric. *(LFI)*

Above: Stomu Yamashta's Go. Left to right: Michael Shrieve, Stomu Yamashta, Klaus Schulze and Steve. *(Island Records)*

Below: Steve collects his Grammy Awards at the Shrine Auditorium, Los Angeles, February 1987. *(LFI)*

Below: On tour, 1988. *(Pictorial Press)*

Above: *(Pictorial Press)*

Above Right: Steve and Genia's two daughters, Mary Clare (top) and Elizabeth Dawn. *(Steve Winwood collection)*

Left: Steve and Genia after their marriage in New York, January, 1987. *(Steve Winwood collection)*

Right: With Genia. *(LFI)*

TER 12

back in the highlife

In May 1988 Steve Winwood released the single 'Roll With It', followed by the album in June, his first on Virgin. There were eight compositions, with lyrics by Will Jennings (one 'Hearts On Fire' was written with Jim Capaldi) which had been recorded in Dublin and Toronto. Musicians on the album included vocalists Tessa Niles and Mark Williamson, Mike Lawler and Robbie Kilgore (keyboards), Paul Pesco (guitar), and percussionist Bashiri Johnson, Jimmy Bralower and John Robinson.

Virgin had signed Steve to a multi-million dollar contract which his manager cheerfully described as "insane". The music had a strong all-American feel, which many welcomed as a return to Winwoodian roots, a feeling emphasised by the use of The Memphis Horns which gave the authentic sound of sixties soul, such an influence on bands like The Spencer Davis Group and their contemporaries. Most of all it just sounded full of joy and exuberance.

Undoubtedly his best, most consistently satisfying solo album, it was also a huge hit and he went back on tour again. The 'Roll With It' world tour sponsored by Michelob opened in St. Louis on July 7, 1988, and went on for 32 dates across America finishing in Buffalo, New York on September 3. Then came his UK concerts, which included a rather chaotic show at Birmingham NEC that was marred by sound problems, and his much more successful eight nights at The Royal Albert Hall.

Said Steve in December 1988 at the end of a fantastic year: "I'm happier than I've ever been, and I have a family which is fantastic. And careerwise, I would never have believed someone who told me 10 years ago I was going to have my biggest record ever when I was 40."

When we talked later he explained that despite all the rationalisation and common sense decisions that were part of launching the new Winwood, he had never altered his deep-felt beliefs about music. "I've never written the stuff to fall into a format because I think that's a mistake and I've never tried to aim for an audience. Although I realise in some people's eyes it seems that I've been making music for the Yuppie CD set! Maybe. I'll leave that sort of concept to the marketing people at the record company. They tend to know more about it."

But Steve did consciously restructure and modernise his music for an eighties audience. "Right. Traffic used to have those rambling long solos and jams, yeah, that's true. I suppose I changed because I *definitely* wanted to reach more people and knew that to go on playing the old way wouldn't help. It's fair enough people saying I got 'commercial' but wanting to reach more people isn't wrong and I felt I had something to offer. It wasn't a compromise. I don't think I started to play watered down jazz to try and do that. I just saw how I could get what I did across to more people. I listened to the radio and heard the kind of things that were happening and felt I could fit in."

Steve didn't sit down one day and ponder over what he could write that could be put alongside Phil Collins or whoever was big in the eighties. But he did draw on his experience from previous decades of Winwood work and utilise the exciting possibilities of new recording techniques.

"The sixties were a period of incredible change, and somehow the music was changing with people's ideas," he says. "They thought then that the music was making social changes, but I never felt it did. The music just accompanied the social changes that were going on. I don't think music changed anything. People's ideas change and the music changes with them. Obviously The Beatles lyrics did affect people greatly but personally I haven't changed in my beliefs. I used to think Lionel Hampton, (the brilliant Vibrophone player) was a great musician in those days and I still do now."

He has changed his opinions about lifestyle and attitudes, which is something that has to be understood by those who perhaps cherish memories of Steve Winwood in the sixties.

"Seeing some of the things that happened, and the way people's lives petered out had a really big effect on me, probably bigger than I might like to admit, y'know. The people who immediately spring to mind are Chris Wood and Jimi Hendrix. And there were others I knew who have died – Rebop, Graham Bond, in addition to the greats like Janis Joplin, Paul Kossoff and John Bonham, some I knew well and some I met briefly. I met them all, including Jim Morrison. As I got older I put music a little bit more into perspective."

Anthony 'Rebop' Kwaku Baah, was Traffic's percussionist and another victim of rock 'n' roll excess. He was given his name by jazz trumpeter Dizzy Gillespie and appeared on such albums as 'Traffic – On The Road' and 'Shoot Out At The Fantasy Factory'. He was born in Ghana and "Of course he was brought up in the jungle, so he had different philosophies and ideas," says Steve. "It affected his whole concept of civilisation. Like Chris Wood, Rebop had a great influence on me. He had a melodic sense which was unusual for a percussionist. He knew the way melodies have their own rhythms. And he taught me a lot about melodic structure."

Steve has travelled widely and taken more of an interest in the world since he was able to get out of the treadmill of touring, when the most he was likely to see of a country was the dressing room wall. "Now I've seen other cultures you see how music is a part of everyday life."

He feels that music should be integrated in a rational way rather than become linked to an excessive, perhaps self-destructive lifestyle, as was typified by the sixties' approach that lingers on today. Musicians were expected to drink heavily and do a lot of drugs, as if their music could not be accepted without their influence and presence.

"That wasn't a good thing. It was based on the Parisian existentialist notion that the artist must suffer to produce something good. I suppose I changed my attitudes in the mid-seventies which was a difficult time and brought a big change for me. You have talked about me undergoing 'frustrations' in that period. Well the truth was everybody still seemed to love me – but I hadn't got any money! People would say nice things like, 'Steve, you're great.' But I wasn't selling any records! That's a very strange situation to be in. People automatically think you are doing great. Then if you do something that ultimately proves successful, some of those people will start to say: 'Oh well, he's sold out.' All I did was maximise my career.

"I'm aware that some stuff I do is better than others. Some of the early Spencer Davis stuff was too contrived perhaps. When I hear the old records, usually by accident, I can't help but listen. I can't hear it as background. I get transported back and remember everything . . . I heard some stuff that Spencer and Muff had from some radio show in Denmark and it brought back memories.

"Things have changed a lot. I'm accused of appealing to Yuppies and the CD crowd. Before that I was probably appealing to the hippies. I don't think my music made them either hippies or yuppies! It's just an evolution.

"When Eliza was born I cut the tour short, but I'm at the stage now where I am not going to tour when family matters come up. That's very important to me. I love being a dad! It's fantastic. The fact that I went to New York for a while in the early eighties was really due to career pressure. It wasn't because I'd had enough of the rural country life. At that time it was important for me to get more outside influences from a musical point of view. But I'm quite happy to be a rural hermit!"

Unlike so many artists who began their careers in the sixties, and burnt themselves out as artists and as people, Steve, by his softly, softly approach and refusal to be rushed, has conserved his energy and talent. His has been no mere 'revival' but a late blooming and it seems certain that the best is yet to come. However he doesn't see himself making albums and touring in perpetuity. As I sat with Steve in the kitchen of the old manor house at two o'clock in the morning, after an evening at the inn, he was in reflective mood. I asked him if he felt that he was a better singer and player now, after all his years of experience, even more so than he'd been during the first flush of youthful fame.

"That's a good question . . . because I know most people don't think I am! But people's memories play tricks on them. They think everything sounded great when they were 21 – and in love. Y'know what I mean? Everything seemed so wonderful then. You can listen to my records from the old days and some of the stuff was great, and some of it was . . . okay. Maybe I had more ability then, but I wasn't so sure how to control or guide it. With Traffic our music was probably a little less accessible than The Spencer Davis Group, and it was perhaps harder to follow the thread of what we were doing. There were a lot of different line-ups and albums but it was probably the most productive era for me, although now I'm using things I learnt in Traffic.

"With 'Roll With It' I certainly did get back to the sort of early records that were an influence on Spencer Davis. I really did want to identify with the old group on that last album. It was a musical statement about The Spencer Davis Group and I think I succeeded with songs like 'Dancing Shoes' and 'Roll With It'. Traffic had something very strong but subtle and in many ways I handled Traffic badly and I was probably wrong to have broken it up. I could have changed the band . . . hindsight is a wonderful thing! But I was totally responsible for the changes within Traffic. I wasn't just happily floating along within it, like maybe I was in bands like Airforce. That band was like a rest period for me."

Steve has always seemed to tolerate a taxing situation for a long time before suddenly snapping and make a swift decision to end things and move on. "Yes that's right. That's exactly what I did with my first marriage. I went along with that which was wrong."

His present situation is far from intolerable, but that doesn't mean Steve Winwood will follow a predictable path in the future. He has another two albums to fulfil his contractual commitments by 1992. The next album is due to be delivered to Virgin in May 1990, and the earliest release date considered is June of the same year. Work on this album began in the spring of 1989. At that point Steve hadn't been in his home studio for nearly two years but he began laying down basic ideas, using his new 64-channel desk.

"After that I'd like to concentrate on some production," says Steve. "I don't see myself touring far into the future. It's okay and something I enjoy, but I can't do that to earn my living any more. It can be a good way to earn a lot of money but it's not the kind of life I want any longer. Because I have a family, I don't want to live like that any more. I'm now 41 and I might do some touring between now and 1992, but I'll be 44 then and I won't be going on the road much after that.

"I want to be passing on my experience, what I've learned, and all my knowledge, to younger musicians."

161

RAPHY

steve winwood discography

SPENCER DAVIS GROUP SINGLES

Dimples/ Sittin' And Thinkin'
Fontana TF 471 August 1964

I Can't Stand It/ Midnight Train
Fontana TF 499 October 1964

Every Little Bit Hurts/ It Hurts Me So
Fontana TF 530 January 1965

Strong Love/ This Hammer
Fontana TF 571 May 1965

Keep On Running/ High Time Baby
Fontana TF 632 November 1965

Somebody Help Me/ Stevie's Blues
Fontana TF 679 March 1966

When I Come Home/ Trampolines
Fontana TF 739 September 1966

Gimme Some Lovin'/ Blues In F
Fontana TF 672 November 1966

I'm A Man/ I Can't Get Enough Of It
Fontana TF 785 January 1967

Gimme Some Lovin'/ Gimme Some Lovin' '76
Island WIP 6318 August 1976

SPENCER DAVIS OVERSEAS SINGLES

Gimme Some Lovin' (alternate take)/
Blues In F
United Artists 50108 (USA) 1966

Det War In Schoeneberg/ Stevie's Groove
Fontana 269 344 TF (Germany) 1966

SPENCER DAVIS EPs

Every Little Bit Hurts
Fontana TE 17450 July 1965

You Put The Hurt On Me
Fontana TE 17444 September 1965.

Sittin' And Thinkin'
Fontana TE 17463 May 1966

Hits Of The Spencer Davis Group
Fontana MCF 5003 (cassette only) July 1967

Keep On Running
Island IEP 10 May 1978

SPENCER DAVIS LPs

Their First Album
Fontana TL 5242 July 1965

Second Album
Fontana TL 5295 February 1966

Autumn '66
Fontana TL 5359 September 1966

Every Little Bit Hurts
Wing WL 1165 July 1967
(re-issue of 'Their First Album')

The Best Of The Spencer Davis Group
Fontana TL 5443/STL 5443 December 1967

The Best Of The Spencer Davis Group
Island ILP 970/ILPS 9070 1969

SPENCER DAVIS COMPILATIONS

Rock Generation Volume 5
BYG 529 705 (France) 1972
Includes live versions of 'Dimples' and 'Night Time Is The Right Time'.

The History Of British Blues
Sire SAS 3701 (USA) 1973
Includes early Mike Vernon demo of 'Mean Ole Frisco'. The remaining titles – 'Dimples', 'Help Me', 'Right Kind Of Loving' and 'You're So Fine' – remain unissued.

TRAFFIC SINGLES

Paper Sun/ Giving To You
Island WIP 6002 May 1967

Hole In My Shoe/ Smiling Phases
Island WIP 6017 August 1967

Here We Go Round The Mulberry Bush/ Coloured Rain
Island WIP 6025 November 1967

No Name No Face No Number/ Roamin' Through the Gloamin' With 40,000 Headmen
Island WIP 6030 February 1968

You Can All Join In/ Withering Tree
Island WIP 6041 August 1968 (cancelled)

Feelin' Alright/ Withering Tree
Island WIP 6041 September 1968

Medicated Goo/ Shanghai Noodle Factory
Island WIP 6050 December 1968

Hole In My Shoe/ Here We Go Round The Mulberry Bush
Island WIP 6199 May 1974

Walking In The Wind/ Walking In The Wind (instrumental)
Island WIP 6207 October 1974

TRAFFIC EPs

Hole In My Shoe
Island IEP 7 December 1967

TRAFFIC LPs

Mr Fantasy
Island ILP 961/ ILPS 9061 December 1967
Also on CD, CID 9061

Traffic
Island ILP 981/ ILPS 9081 October 1968
Also on CD, CID 9081

Last Exit
Island ILPS 9097 May 1969
Also on CD, CID 9097

The Best Of Traffic
Island ILPS 9112 October 1969

John Barleycorn Must Die
Island ILPS 9116 July 1970
Also on CD, CID 9116

Traffic Live
Island ILPS 9142 1970
Cancelled after test pressings were made

Welcome To The Canteen
Island ILPS 9166 September 1971
Also on CD, CID 9166

The Low Spark Of High Heeled Boys
Island ILPS 9180 November 1971
Also on CD, CID 9180

Shoot Out At The Fantasy Factory
Island ILPS 9224 April 1973
Also on CD, CID 9224

On The Road
Island ISLP 2 October 1973
Also on CD, CIDD 2

Where The Eagle Flies
Island ILPS 9273 September 1974

TRAFFIC COMPILATION

Here We Go Round The Mulberry Bush
United Artists ULP/ SULP 1186 Nov. 1967

BLIND FAITH SINGLE

Change Of Address (instrumental)
Island (unnumbered) 1969
Promotional only

BLIND FAITH LPs

Blind Faith
Polydor 583 059 September 1969

Blind Faith
RSO 2394 142 June 1977 (reissue)

Blind Faith
Polydor 825 094-2 April 1986
CD reissue with two extra tracks

STEVE WINWOOD

BLIND FAITH COMPILATION

Crossroads
Polydor 835 261-1 April 1988
Eric Clapton compilation, with one previously unissued track 'Sleeping In The Ground'.

STEVE WINWOOD SINGLES

Time Is Running Out/ Penultimate Zone
Island WIP 6394 June 1977

While You See A Chance/ Vacant Chair
Island WIP 6555 December 1980

While You See A Chance/ Vacant Chair
Island IPR 2040 (12") December 1980

While You See A Chance/ Vacant Chair
Island CWIP 6555 (cassingle) February 1981

Spanish Dancer (remix)/ Hold On
Island WIP 6680 March 1981

Spanish Dancer (remix)/ Hold On
Island 12WIP 6680 (12") March 1981

Night Train/ Night Train (instrumental)
Island WIP 6710 September 1981

Night Train/ Night Train (instrumental)
Island 12WIP 6680 (12") September 1981

There's A River/ Two Way Stretch
Island WIP 6747 November 1981

Still In The Game/ Dust
Island WIP 6786 July 1982

Valerie/ Slowdown Sundown
Island WIP 6818 September 1982

Valerie/ Slowdown Sundown
Island 12WIP 6818 (12") September 1982

Your Silence Is Your Song/ Your Silence Is Your Song (instrumental)
Island WIP 6849 June 1983

Higher Love/ And I Go
Island IS 288 June 1986

Higher Love (extended)/ Higher Love (instrumental)/ And I Go
Island 12IS 288 (12") June 1986

Higher Love/ And I Go/ Valerie/ While You See A Chance/ Talking Back To The Night
Island CIS 288 (cassingle) June 1986

Freedom Overspill/ Spanish Dancer
Island IS 294 August 1986
Initial copies came with free interview cassette

Freedom Overspill (Liberty mix)/ Freedom Overspill (LP version)/ Spanish Dancer
sland 12IS 294 (12") August 1986
Initial copies came in fold-out sleeve with free 7" single, 'Low Spark Of High Heeled Boys'/ 'Gimme Some Lovin'.

Freedom Overspill/ Spanish Dancer/ Higher Love/ And I Go
Island ISD 294 (double-pack) August 1986

Back In The High Life Again/ Help Me Angel
Island IS 303 January 1987

Back In The High Life Again/ Night Train (instrumental)/ Help Me Angel
Island 12IS 303 (12") January 1987

Valerie (remix)/ Talking Back To the Night (instrumental)
Island IS 336 September 1987

Valerie (remix)/ Talking Back To The Night (instrumental)/ The Finer Things
Island 12IS 336 (12") September 1987

Valerie (remix)/ Talking Back To the Night (instrumental)/ The Finer Things
Island CIS 336 (cassingle) September 1987

Roll With It/ The Morning Side
Virgin VS 1085 May 1988

Roll With It (12" mix)/ The Morning Side
Virgin VST 1085 (12") May 1988

Don't You Know What The Night Can Do (remix)/ Don't You Know What The Night Can Do (instrumental)
Virgin VS 1107 August 1988

Don't You Know What The Night Can Do (extended remix)/ Don't You Know What The Night Can Do (instrumental)
Virgin VST 1107 (12") 1107 August 1988

Holding On/ Holding On (instrumental)
Virgin VS 1135 October 1988

Holding On/ Holding On (instrumental)
Virgin VST 1135 (12") October 1988

STEVE WINWOOD CD SINGLES

Valerie
Island CID 336 September 1987

Roll With It
Virgin VSCD 1085 May 1988

Don't You Know What The Night Can Do
Virgin VSCD 1107 August 1988

STEVE WINWOOD LPs

Steve Winwood
Island ILPS 9494 July 1977
Also on CD, CID 9494

Arc Of A Diver
Island ILPS 9576 December 1980
Also on CD, CID 9576

Talking Back To The Night
Island ILPS 9777 September 1982
Also on CD, CID 9777

Back In The High Life
Island ILPS 9844 July 1986
Also on CD, CID 9844

Chronicles
Island SSW 1 October 1987
Also on CD, SSWCD 1

Roll With It
Virgin V 2532 June 1988
Also CD, CDV 2532

STEVE WINWOOD COMPILATIONS

Winwood
United Artists 9964 1972
US compilation of pre-solo Winwood material

Winwood And Friends
Springboard SPB 4040 1972
US compilation of pre-solo Winwood material

They Call That An Accident
Island ISTA 2 March 1983
Film soundtrack including Winwood's 'Your Silence Is Your Song'

A Conversation With Steve Winwood
Island white label promo
UK promo LP

GUEST APPEARANCES

With Anglos
Incense/ You're Fooling Me
Brit WI 1004 1965
(Reissued in 1965 as Sue WI 4033, again in 1965 as Fontana TF 589 and again in 1969 as Island WIP 6061)

With John Mayall and Steve Anglo
Raw Blues
Ace Of Clubs ACL/SCL 1967
Includes Winwood on 'Long Night'

With Eric Clapton and Powerhouse
Good Time Music
Elektra EUK 260 1967
Includes three tracks by Eric Clapton and The Powerhouse featuring Winwood, 'I Want To Know', 'Steppin' Out' and 'Crossroads'. LP later reissued as 'What's Shakin''.

With Ginger Baker's Airforce
Man Of Constant Sorrow/ Doin' It
Polydor 56380 March 1970

With Stomu Yamashta's Go
Crossing The Line (live)/ Winner Loser (live)
Island 12WIP 6444 (12″ only) May 1978

SESSION WORK

Jimi Hendrix
Electric Ladyland
Track 613 008/009, CD: 823 359-2 1968

Joe Cocker
With A Little Help From My Friends
Regal Zonophone SLRZ 1006 1969

Gordon Jackson
Thinking Back
Marmalade 608 012 1969

Ginger Baker's Airforce
Ginger Baker's Airforce
Polydor 2662 001 1970

Jimi Hendrix
Cry Of Love
Polydor 2302 023 1970

McDonald And Giles
McDonald And Giles
Island ILPS 9126 1970

Shawn Phillips
Contribution
A&M AMLS 978 1970

Leon Russell
Leon Russell
A&M AMLS 982 1970

Howlin' Wolf
London Sessions
Rolling Stones COC 49101 1971

STEVE WINWOOD

Reg King
United Artists UAS 29157 1971

Rebop Kwaku Baah
Rebop
Island SW 9304, US only 1972

Jim Capaldi
Oh How We Danced
Island ILPS 9187 1972

The Sutherland Brothers
Lifeboat
Island ILPS 9212 1972

Various Artists
Tommy
Ode SP 88001 1972

Muddy Waters
London Sessions
Chess 6310 121 1972

Blondel
Blondel
Island ILPS 9257 1973

Eric Clapton
Rainbow Concert
RSO 2394 116, CD: Polydor 831 320-2 1973

Alvin Lee and Mylon Lefevre
Road To Freedom
Chrysalis CAS 1054 1973

John Martyn
Inside Out
Island ILPS 9253 1973

Shawn Phillips
Faces
A&M AMLS 64363 1973

Lou Reed
Berlin
RCA RS 1002, CD: PD 84388 1973

Third World
Aiye Keta
Island HELP 14 1973

Jim Capaldi
Whale Meat Again
Island ILPS 9254 1974

Viv Stanshall
Man Opening Umbrellas Ahead
Warners K 56062 1974

Muddy Waters
London Revisited
Chess 60026, US only 1974

Jim Capaldi
Short Cut Draw Blood
Island ILPS 9336 1975

Jade Warrior
Waves
Island ILPS 9318 1975

Fania All-Stars
Delicate And Jumpy
Island ILPS 9447 1976

Toots And The Maytals
Reggae Got Soul
Island ILPS 9374 1976

Stomu Yamashta's Go
Go
Island ILPS 9387 1976

Stomu Yamashta's Go
Go Live From Paris
Island ISLD 10 1976

Sandy Denny
Rendezvous
Island ILPS 9433 1977

John Martyn
One World
Island ILPS 9492, CD: CID 9492 1977

Julie Covington
Julie Covington
Virgin V 2107 1978

I Jahman
Haile I Hymn
Island ILPS 9521 1978

Viv Stanshall
Sir Henry At Rawlinson End
Charisma CAS 1139 1978

Marianne Faithfull
Broken English
Island ILPS 9570, CD: CID 9570 1979

Gong
Downwind
Arista SPART 1080 1979

George Harrison
George Harrison
Dark Horse K 56562 1979

Marianne Faithfull
Dangerous Acquaintances
Island ILPS 9648 1981

Viv Stanshall
Teddy Boys Don't Knit
Charisma CAS 1153 1981

Talk Talk
Colour of Spring
EMI EMC 3506

STEVE WINWOOD